The Litany of
THE SACRED HEART

The Litany of
THE SACRED HEART

By Rev. A. Biskupek, S.V.D.

THE BRUCE PUBLISHING COMPANY
MILWAUKEE

IMPRIMI POTEST:
LAWRENCE G. MACK, S.V.D.
Superior provincialis

NIHIL OBSTAT:
JOHN A. SCHULIEN, S.T.D.
Censor librorum

IMPRIMATUR:
✠ALBERT G. MEYER
Archiepiscopus Milwauchiensis
January 23, 1956

BX 2157
B62

Rosary College Dewey Classification Number: 242

Library of Congress Catalog Card Number: 56–7033

Contents

v

The Litany of
THE SACRED HEART

The Call of Love

DEVOTION to the Sacred Heart of Jesus may be said to be as old as Christianity. The words used by the beloved disciple to record the piercing of the side of Christ are an invitation to God-loving souls to enter into that Sacred Heart as the dwelling place of His boundless love. "One of the soldiers opened his side with a lance, and immediately there came out blood and water" (Jn. 19:34). Among the early Fathers we find numerous passages which set forth the profound significance of this event and reveal their own grateful love and devotion to the Sacred Heart of Jesus. The breviary readings for the octave of the feast of the Sacred Heart are taken from SS. Augustine, John Chrysostom, Gregory the Great, Cyril of Alexandria. And it is but natural that the opened side of the Redeemer should arouse loving attention among mystics of the Middle Ages. Thus we have saints like Bonaventure, Bernard, Bernardine, Mechtildis, and especially Gertrude, all absorbed in the contemplation of the love of the Sacred Heart.

St. Margaret Mary

But only within the past centuries has public devotion to the Sacred Heart come into prominence, and that especially through the efforts of St. John Eudes. This saint is justly called the author of the liturgical cult of the Sacred Hearts of Jesus and Mary. However, in order to bring the cult of the Sacred Heart of Jesus to its full and perfect development and to propagate it

1

throughout the world, God chose as His instrument a humble virgin of the Order of the Visitation, St. Margaret Mary Alacoque. In frequent apparitions our Lord made known to her the riches and the desires of His divine Heart. The most famous of these apparitions took place in 1674 and 1675.

In the first of these apparitions, spring, 1674, Jesus allowed the saint to rest her head upon His breast. He then said to her, "My divine heart is so full of love for men, and for thee in particular, that being unable to contain within itself the flames of its ardent charity, it must needs spread them abroad by thy efforts. My heart desires to manifest itself to men, that they may be enriched with its treasures which I reveal to thee, and which contain graces of sanctification and salvation, necessary to withdraw their souls from perdition. I have chosen thee, in spite of thy unworthiness and ignorance for the accomplishment of this great design, so that all may be done by me."

In the second apparition, some time later, Jesus appeared to the saint, resplendent with glory, with His five wounds shining like brilliant suns. Flames issued on all sides from His sacred body, but especially from His breast, which resembled a furnace. In this He showed her His most adorable Heart, the living sun of these flames. Then He disclosed to her to what an excess He had carried His love for men, from whom He received only ingratitude. His words were, "This I feel more deeply than all that I suffered in my passion. If they would return me love for love, I should think but little of all that I have suffered for them, and should wish, if it were possible, to suffer still more. But instead of love I meet with coldness and repulses on every side in return for all my eagerness to do them good. Do thou at least console me, by supplying for their ingratitude as far as thou art able." Our Lord then prescribed the manner in which Sister Margaret Mary was to do this. She was to receive Holy Communion as often as obedience would allow her, especially on the first Friday of each month. Every Thursday night she was to observe the hour before midnight as a holy hour, subject also to obedience. He said, "Every Thursday I will make thee participate in the mortal sadness which it was my will to feel in the Garden of Olives, and this sadness will reduce thee to an agony harder to bear than death. To bear me company in the humble prayer, which I offered to my Father in my anguish, thou shalt rise between eleven o'clock and midnight and remain prostrate with me for an hour, thy face to the ground, so as to appease the divine anger of my Father by begging pardon for sinners, as well as to share, and in some way to soften, the bitterness I felt in being at that time abandoned by my apostles, an abandonment which obliged me to reproach them with not having been able to watch one hour with me."

The third apparition took place on the feast of St. John the Apostle, December 27, 1674. The saint herself gives the following account of this apparition: "The divine heart was represented to me as on a throne of fire and flames shedding rays of light on every side, brighter than the sun and transparent as crystal. The wound which he had received on the cross was clearly visible. A crown of thorns encircled the divine heart and it was surmounted by a cross. My divine Savior made me understand that these instruments of his passion were symbols, that his immense love for men had been the source of all his sufferings and humiliations endured for us. From the first moment of his incarnation all these torments and this ignominy had been present to him, and in order to prove his love for us he had accepted all the humiliations, poverty, and sufferings that his sacred humanity was to endure during his whole mortal life, and also all the outrages to which his love would expose him in the Blessed Sacrament of the altar." Then our Lord made her understand that it was His great desire to be loved by men that had prompted Him to manifest His Heart to them so that all might be enriched with the divine treasures of which His Sacred Heart is the source. Lastly, He assured the saint that He would be pleased to be honored under the representation of a heart of flesh, that He even desired such representations to become public, so that men might be touched by its sight. He promised that He would pour forth the gifts of His love abundantly on all those who would honor His Heart, and that wherever the image of His Heart should be exposed for special veneration it would draw down every sort of blessing. The saint understood that this devotion was a last effort of divine love to draw men of these latter times to love Him in return.

The octave of the feast of Corpus Christi was chosen by our Lord for what was perhaps the most important and is certainly the best known of the revelations. Showing the saint His divine Heart He said, "Behold this heart which has so loved men, that it has spared nothing, even to exhausting and consuming itself to prove to them its love. In return I receive from the greater number nothing but ingratitude, contempt, irreverence, sacrilege, and coldness in this sacrament of my love. But what I feel still more is that there are hearts consecrated to me, who treat me thus." Our Lord then asked for a feast in honor of His Sacred Heart to be celebrated on the first Friday after the octave of Corpus Christi and referred the saint to Father Claude de la Colombière, S.J., for assistance in carrying out this task.

Growth and Triumph

Through the efforts of St. Margaret Mary and her spiritual directors, Father Claude de la Colombière and Father Croiset, both of the Society of Jesus, the devotion to the Sacred Heart spread rapidly, especially among the Sisters of the Visitation Order, of which St. Margaret was a member, and in the Society of Jesus. However, efforts to bring about a positive ecclesiastical approval through the institution of a feast in honor of the Sacred Heart were unsuccessful for a long time. Renewed petitions, and particularly a memorandum submitted by the bishops of Poland, influenced Pope Clement XIII, in 1765, to grant a feast with a proper Office and Mass, first only for Poland and for the Roman Archconfraternity. In rapid succession, however, the celebration of the feast was petitioned and granted for an ever increasing number of dioceses and religious communities. Pius IX then made it a major double feast for the universal Church in 1856; Leo XIII raised it to the rank of a double of the first class, and Pius XI finally added an octave in 1928. Pius XI also ordered a new Office to be composed and prescribed that on the feast itself the act of reparation be recited in all churches throughout the world. The spread of the devotion to the Sacred Heart, in spite of long, persistent, and violent opposition, is a clear indication that the hand of God has done the work. It has become one of the most popular devotions; there is scarcely a church or chapel without some representation of the Sacred Heart of Jesus, and the observance of the first Friday and the holy hour has become almost universal.

Significance for Our Times

St. Gertrude once asked our Lord why the devotion to His Sacred Heart had not been given to the world through St. John, who had such a profound understanding of the love of his divine Master. She received the answer that this devotion had been reserved for a later period, when charity would grow cold and the world would need the divine fire to be inflamed again. Against this background the characterization which Pope Pius XI gave of our times in his encyclical *Miserentissimus Redemptor* is striking, "From every side there comes to us the cry of afflicted peoples, whose princes and leaders have indeed risen and come together against the Lord and against His Church. But a cause of grief is likewise the fact that among the faithful themselves, who have been cleansed by the blood of the immaculate Lamb in Baptism and have been made rich in grace, so many men of every station in life are found who suffer from an unbelievable ignorance of things divine and are infected by false doctrines. They live a life far from their Father's house, enmeshed in vice, which neither the light of the true faith illumines nor the hope of a future life delights. Nor does it refresh and foster the fervor of charity, so that they seem truly to sit in the darkness and the shadow of death. On top of all these evils as it were there comes the sloth and indifference of those, who like the sleeping and fleeing disciples waver in faith and woefully forsake Christ oppressed by sorrow and surrounded by the satellites of satan; then the perfidy of those, who following the example of the traitor Judas either recklessly and sacrilegiously partake of the altar, or pass over into the camp of the enemy. And thus there comes to mind even against our will the thought that the times are approaching of which our Lord has foretold, 'And because iniquity has abounded, the charity of many shall grow cold.' "

This explains why the devotion to the Sacred Heart was reserved for our times, but for that very reason it is also the sign of hope and victory through which the world will be renewed in the charity of Christ. So thought Pope Pius XI, "Once upon a time God willed the rainbow to appear in the clouds for the men that came out of the Ark of Noe; it was to be the sign of a new covenant of friendship. In like manner did Jesus in His love show the nations His most Sacred Heart, as it were, a raised banner of peace and charity, a certain guarantee of victory in warfare. . . . It was then a pertinent statement which our predecessor, Leo XIII, of happy memory, made in his encyclical *Annum sacrum*, when, struck by the opportuneness of the devotion to the Sacred Heart of Jesus, he did not hesitate to say, 'When in the time of her beginning the Church was oppressed by the yoke of the Caesars, there appeared to the youthful emperor high in the air a cross, the harbinger and pledge of victory which soon followed. Behold, now in our days proposed to us another most auspicious and divine sign: the most Sacred Heart of Jesus, surmounted by a cross shining amid flames with brightest splendor. In that Heart we must place all our hope, from It we must implore and expect the salvation of men.' " The reason for such hope is found in the very object of the devotion and the special features of its practice.

Object of Devotion

The first and immediate object of the devotion is the physical Heart of Jesus. Apart from any other consideration It deserves our love and adoration as part of our Lord's human nature hypostatically united with the second Person of the Blessed Trinity.

Moreover, the heart is one of the most excellent and necessary organs of the body. It is the source of the blood that supplies the vital energy for any activity, and it is most intimately affected by human emotions, love, hope, joy, fear. The faster or slower pulse, the pale or red color of the checks, give evidence of the influence of the emotions upon the heart. Applying this to the Heart of Jesus we see that It is the source of the precious blood, the price of our redemption; it furnished the physical energy which enabled Jesus to carry out His mission and had an intimate part in all those deep and holy emotions which Jesus experienced in His prayer, His labors, and sufferings. How much do we not owe to this Sacred Heart! It surely deserves our grateful veneration and love.

But the heart is also the symbol of love. Love is the driving power in man's life and more than any other factor does it affect the heart. Holy Scripture, too, adopts this symbolism of love. Thus the great commandment, which God announced to His people on Mount Sinai and which our Lord solemnly restated, is that we must love God with our whole heart. All virtue and holiness of life are rooted in love so that the perfect observance of the commandment of love is the observance of the whole law. Love implies the practice of all virtues, whereas the absence of love excludes the perfection of any and every virtue.

St. Augustine develops this thought as follows, "The apostle Paul, wishing to commend the fruit of the Spirit against the works of the flesh, put this at the head: The fruit of the Spirit is charity. Then he adds the other fruits, as it were, springing from and joined with charity; they are joy, peace, longanimity, benignity, goodness, faith, meekness, continence, chastity. And truly, who rejoices with genuine joy, if not he who loves the good whence all joy proceeds? With whom can we have true peace, unless it be with him whom we truly love? Who is patient, persevering in good works, unless he be fervent through love? Who is kind, unless he love him whom he assists? Who is good, unless he has become such through love? Who believes unto salvation if not by faith that operates through love? Who is really meek, unless love restrains him? Who abstains from things disgraceful, unless he loves the things by which he is made honorable? Rightly, therefore, does the good Master commend charity so frequently as if it were the only thing to be prescribed.

Without it all other good works yield no profit, and, on the other hand, it cannot be held in possession except by the practice of all virtues which make a man perfect" (Feast of SS. Simon and Jude, Oct. 28).

Thus the Heart of Jesus stands before us as the symbol of our Saviour's all-exceeding, undying love. Love was the driving power of His whole life. Love drew Him from the bosom of the Father to this earth. Love prompted Him to choose a life of poverty, privations, labors, and sufferings. Love led Him in quest of the lost sheep. Love nailed Him to the cross. Love keeps Him in the blessed Eucharist, for, having loved His own who were in the world, He loved them to the end.

Summing up what has been said we can thus state the Catholic doctrine on this point: The object of the devotion to the Sacred Heart of Jesus is the physical Heart of our Saviour, not, however, separated from His Person but united with Him. This Heart symbolizes His love which is the determining factor of His life and holiness and the entire work of our redemption. Hence the ultimate object of this devotion is the Person of our Blessed Saviour under the special aspect of His love, Jesus, the divine Lover of God and of souls.

Practice of Devotion

Love

The practice of devotion to the Sacred Heart is essentially the practice of the love of God and men. The test of the love of God is the observance of the commandments, the joyful and generous doing of the will of God; the test of the love of men is above all zeal for their salvation.

Jesus loves the Father and therefore the goal of His life and His daily meat is to do the will of the Father. "Behold, I come to do thy will. . . . Yes, Father, for such was thy good pleasure. . . . Not as I will, but as thou willest" — these are the high lights revealing the love of the Father burning in the Sacred Heart of Jesus.

Jesus loves souls and therefore He comes down from heaven for us and our salvation; He shows us the ways of salvation by word and example, and in the end pays the price of our ransom in His blood. He seeks the lost sheep and dies for us that we might live.

Such love of God and men stands in glaring contrast to the widespread apostasy from God that we witness in the world, the rebellion against the moral law, the frightful reign of passion, hatred, lust, and greed. Devotion to the Sacred Heart, and that is the practice of the love of God and of men, is the remedy for these evils. Both these loves will find their expression in the fervent, generous, apostolic life of the faithful. Love will teach us to think not only of ourselves but of the great intentions of the Sacred Heart of Jesus. We shall pray for the conversion of pagans and sinners, for the return of our separated brethren, for peace among the nations, for the Catholic education of the young, for an increase of priestly and religious vocations, for the success of any and every enterprise that has for its object the extension of the kingdom of Christ and the salvation of souls. And not only by prayer but even more shall we prove our love through the practice of those virtues which are so dear to the Heart of our Saviour. Humility will foster esteem and respect for our fellow men, meekness will bear with their faults and failings, charity will come to their assistance in their needs. There is nothing that draws men as effectively to God as the charity practiced for His sake by His followers. Thus quietly and unobtrusively men are made captives of the love of the Sacred Heart.

Atonement

According to Pope Pius XI, "The spirit of expiation, in particular of reparation, has always held the principal place in the cult of the Sacred Heart of Jesus, and there is nothing more in harmony with its origin, nature, practices, and virtues which are proper to this devotion." The Offertory verse of the feast of the Sacred Heart of Jesus, taken from the 68th psalm, recalls the desire of the Sacred Heart for companionship in the atonement which He rendered for the sins of men, "My heart hath expected reproach and misery, and I looked for one that would grieve together with me and there was none; and I sought one that would console me and I found none." It was the same touching complaint which our Saviour addressed to St. Margaret Mary that for all His love He received only coldness and indifference and offenses from so many men, even from souls consecrated to Him.

The answer to our Saviour's complaint is atonement, acts of virtue that make reparation for the offense of sin; it is inseparable from true love of Jesus. Such atonement is the holy hour that our Lord asked St. Margaret Mary to keep during the midnight hour from Thursday to Friday. It is also the act of reparation to be recited on the feast of the Sacred Heart by order of Pope Pius XI. By our intention we can make any good work an act of atonement, but it is surely fitting that, in view of the evils of the times, we make efforts to atone by acts which are directly opposed to the sins by which God is offended. Thus we can offer Him frequent acts of love for the coldness and indifference of the world, absolute submission to His will in all things in place of the self-will and contempt of divine authority prevalent in our days, works of mortification in place of the pleasure seeking which is the cause of innumerable sins. As love prompted the Sacred Heart of Jesus to make Himself the Lamb of God that takes away the sins of the world by His sacrifice on the cross, so love will urge the disciples of the Crucified to make themselves victim souls through daily self-immolation, thus to offer reparation to the offended majesty of God and to lift the burden of sin from the world.

The Blessed Eucharist

It is significant that all the apparitions of the Sacred Heart of Jesus to St. Margaret Mary took place in the presence of the Blessed Sacrament. In this sacrament Jesus is present really, truly, and substantially; here is the Heart that beats for us, the Heart that was pierced for us; here the blood that was shed for our salvation. Here we have the memorial of all His wonderful works. Calvary with its mystery of love is transplanted upon the altar in every holy Mass, but also heaven with all the glory of our risen Saviour, who having died once now dies no more and to the end of days remains our Emmanuel, God in the midst of His people. Here we can come close to Him, see and taste how sweet is His presence; here we can watch Him with the eye of faith in the continuation of His saving mission. Here we can learn from Him to be poor, obedient, patient, and long-suffering. Here burns the love that must fill our hearts with the desire to make atonement, love that is strong as death and can set on fire a world that is cold as ice. Devotion to the Sacred Heart necessarily leads to the Blessed Sacrament, because love aims at union, friendship, companionship, at oneness of mind and heart, and all this is offered to us in the Blessed Eucharist.

And so there is hope for a renewal of the world in the Spirit of Christ in spite of all its wickedness. Says Pope Pius XI,

"Where sin has abounded, grace has abounded more. As the perversity of men is increased, there also grows under the inspiration of the Holy Spirit the number of the faithful of both sexes, who seek with so much the more fervor to render satisfaction to the divine Heart for so many injuries inflicted upon It; they even do not hesitate to offer themselves as victims to Christ. And truly, if anyone lovingly considers in his heart what we have mentioned up to now and fixes it deeply upon his soul, the result will be that he not only shrinks from and abstains from every sin as the greatest evil, and abandons himself entirely to the will of God, but he will also strive to repair the violated honor of the divine majesty by continuous prayer, by voluntary mortifications, by the patient endurance of trials that may befall him, and by devoting his whole life to the work of expiation."

The Litany

The Litany of the Sacred Heart of Jesus as we have it now is a combination of two other litanies. One of these was composed by Father Croiset, S.J., who was probably influenced by Sister Magdalen Joly of the Visitation Order, a contemporary of St. Margaret Mary familiar with the revelations and apparitions of the Sacred Heart. Sister Magdalen had composed some prayers and a litany. Another Visitation Sister, Venerable Anne Magdalen Remusat, living at Marseille at the beginning of the eighteenth century, also composed a litany for the members of a confraternity of the Sacred Heart which she founded. This litany consisted of 27 invocations, some taken from the litany of Sister Magdalen Joly and the rest from the litany of Father Croiset, S.J.

A terrible plague raged at Marseille in 1720 and this litany was chanted during public penitential processions. It became quite popular and remained so until the end of the nineteenth century. At that time the Holy See forbade the public recital of all litanies not approved by the Sacred Congregation. Cardinal Perraud, Bishop of Autun, the diocese in which St. Margaret Mary had lived and died, now petitioned the Holy See to approve a litany of the Sacred Heart for public use and at the same time submitted the old litany as composed by Sister Magdalen Remusat. The Sacred Congregation examined the litany, added to it six more invocations from the litany of Father Croiset, in honor of the 33 years of our Saviour's earthly life, and in this form approved it for public use in the diocese of Autun and Marseille and the Order of the Visitation. This was in 1898. At that time Pope Leo XIII had resolved to consecrate the whole human race to the Sacred Heart of Jesus at the beginning of the new century, and to render the event more solemn he approved the Litany of the Sacred Heart of Jesus for public use in the universal Church.

The litany is a veritable compendium of the teaching of the Church on Christ, His person and His work. For this reason the following reflections on the invocations of the litany will help to give the faithful a profounder knowledge of Christ and greater zeal in the imitation of His holy life.

Our times clamor for a prompt and genuine return to God and a deepening of the religious spirit, the mobilization of all spiritual resources. Among the latter, devotion to the Sacred Heart of Jesus undoubtedly holds a prominent place. Its loving appeal, it would appear, has now entered its final stage in our Lady of Fatima's call to prayer and penance and imitation of the virtues of her immaculate Heart. She adds the appeal of her motherly love to the appeal of Jesus' Sacred Heart and offers her suppliant powers to assist in the world's return to Christ, its Saviour and King. May the Heart of Jesus live then in the hearts of men!

1. HEART OF JESUS
Son of the Eternal Father

THE very first invocation of the litany opens up the heavens, as it were, and shows us the mystery of divine life in the bosom of the Most Blessed Trinity. It is the mystery spoken of in the Nicene Creed, when we profess our faith in "one Lord Jesus Christ, the only-begotten Son of God, born of the Father before all ages; God of God, Light of Light, true God of true God; begotten, not made; consubstantial with the Father." Why is Jesus called the Son of the eternal Father? God is a spirit and a process like human generation is absolutely impossible in Him. Here we have to deal, therefore, with a spiritual, divine generation.

Son
A man is the son of his parents because through them he received his human nature. So does the second Person of the Most Blessed Trinity receive His divine nature from the first Person, and that in an infinitely more perfect manner. In human generation the child receives only the body from its parents, God Himself directly and immediately creating the soul. The human nature thus produced is numerically distinct from that of the parents; there are as many human natures as there are human persons. In the divine generation the Father gives His own divine nature to the Son, and, since there is but one divine nature, the Son is also numerically the same God as the Father, the only difference between them being that the Father is the giver and the Son the recipient of this divine nature.

15

St. Paul calls Jesus the image of the Father's substance, that is, the image, in which the Father sees Himself just as He is; but this is possible only if He is equal to the Father in all the infinite perfection of the same divine nature. So it is, and therefore Jesus could answer the request of the Apostle Philip to show them the Father by saying, "He who sees me also sees the father" (Jn. 14:9).

Eternal

God is eternal, without beginning and without end; there is no change in God and what He does now He does from all eternity. Hence He begets the Son eternally; He is the eternal Father and the Son is the eternal Son. Holy Church recalls this thought most impressively in her Christmas liturgy, when she celebrates the birth of our Saviour according to the flesh. The Introit of the first Mass begins with the words, "The Lord has said to me: thou art my Son, today I have begotten thee." For the eternal God there is only today, no yesterday and no tomorrow. The Epistle and Gospel of the third Mass dwell on the majesty, eternity, and omnipotence of the divine Infant in the manger, because the Son of the Virgin Mother is also the Son of the eternal Father. Hence the divine love burning in the Sacred Heart of Jesus has been burning in the bosom of the Trinity from all eternity: "I have loved thee with an everlasting love; therefore I have drawn thee, taking pity on thee" (Jer. 31:3).

Firstborn

St. Paul calls Jesus "the firstborn of every creature" (Col. 1:15); and again, "the firstborn from the dead" (Col. 1:18). The words give us a glimpse into the stupendous wisdom of the divine decree of man's redemption, in which the Sacred Heart of Jesus shines in all Its majesty. The Son of the eternal Father was to assume human nature. But human nature comprises within itself all orders of created things, inanimate and animate, sensitive and spiritual; they were all created that they might meet in the God-Man and in Him be lifted up to their Creator. This is the idea expressed by the great Apostle when he writes, "For in him were created all things in the heavens and on earth, things visible and things invisible. . . . All things have been created through him and unto him, . . . he is before all creatures, and in him all things hold together" (Col. 1:16). So it would have been if men had never sinned. However, even sin cannot change this purpose of creation, but only calls forth a yet grander manifestation of divine wisdom, power, and love. The Firstborn of every creature now becomes the Firstborn from the dead. The Son of the eternal Father now becomes man's Saviour as well. He suffers and dies to atone for their sins that by dying He might conquer death. Then, as the Head of all mankind, He rises from the dead and offers to all the redeemed a share in His life. "Do you not know that all we who have been baptized into Christ Jesus have been baptized into his death? For we were buried with him by means of baptism into death, in order that, just as Christ has arisen from the dead through the glory of the Father, so we also may walk in newness of life" (Rom. 6:3 f.).

Adopted Sons

Incorporation into Christ and participation in His life makes us also the sons of God, even though only adopted sons. So St. Paul can write to the Romans, "You have received a spirit of adoption as sons, by virtue of which we cry, 'Abba, Father!' The Spirit Himself gives testimony to our spirit that we are sons of God" (Rom. 8:16 f.). This divine adoption is the basis of our Christian dignity, a proof of divine love so great that the beloved disciple never tires of recalling it to the faithful, "Behold what manner of love the Father has bestowed upon us, that we should be called children of God; and such we are" (1 Jn. 3:1).

But if we are lifted up to such an exalted dignity as to be the children of God, brothers and sisters of the Son of the eternal Father, is it not a postulate of sound reason as well as of grateful love, that we should prove ourselves worthy of our Christian calling? Jesus Himself exhorts us to be perfect as our Father in heaven is perfect and points to His own life as the example of such perfection. He is meek and humble of heart, seeks nothing but the honor of the Father and always does the things pleasing to the Father. And the Apostle pleads, "Have this mind in you which was also in Christ Jesus" (Phil. 2:5). This is also the petition of holy Church on Christmas Day, "that we may be found in the form of him, in whom our nature is united with thee." The glory of the children of God will be ours to the extent that we have assumed the form of Jesus, the Son of the eternal Father, "For those whom he has foreknown, he has also predestined to be conformed to the image of his Son, that he should be the Firstborn among many brethren" (Rom. 8:29).

2. HEART OF JESUS

Formed by the Holy Ghost in the Womb of the Virgin Mother

ONE of the most venerable churches in the Holy Land is the Church of the Annunciation at Nazareth. From the body of the church a flight of stairs leads down to a grotto. There stands the altar of the Annunciation, in front of which five silver lamps are kept burning constantly. On the floor beneath the altar table a rose is laid out in mosaic and in back of it, flanked by two suspended lamps, an inscription announces the tremendous mystery: "*Verbum caro hic factum est* — Here the Word was made flesh." This is the place in which the Sacred Heart of Jesus was formed by the Holy Spirit in the womb of the Virgin Mother.

The Annunciation

St. Luke, in the first chapter of his Gospel, relates the event as he most probably had learned it from the Mother of Jesus herself, "The angel Gabriel was sent from God to a town of Galilee called Nazareth to a virgin betrothed to a man named Joseph, of the house of David, and the Virgin's name was Mary." Gabriel means power of God, and the grandest manifestation of divine power is to take place. The prince of heaven greets the Virgin with profoundest respect, "Hail, full of grace, the Lord is with thee, blessed art thou among women." The humble Virgin is profoundly stirred — full of grace, blessed among women: what does it all mean? The angel continues, "Do not be afraid, Mary, for thou hast found grace with God. And behold, thou shalt conceive in thy womb and shalt bring forth a son, and thou shalt call his name Jesus. . . ." But how shall all this be done, since Mary had vowed her virginity to the Lord and is certain that this vow had been pleasing to Him? Again the angel gives the answer, "The Holy Spirit shall come upon thee and the power of the Most High shall overshadow thee; and therefore the Holy One to be born shall be called the Son of God." All fear and uncertainty have vanished and Mary humbly accepts what will be her greatest honor, but also the source of sorrow great as the sea. Her answer is, "Behold the handmaid of the Lord; be it done to me according to thy word." In that moment the Word was made flesh. Centuries before that moment Isaias had prophesied, "Behold a virgin shall conceive and bear a Son, and his name shall be called Emmanuel" (Isa. 7:14). The prophecy has now been fulfilled.

Virgin and Mother

Emmanuel has taken up His abode among men and a virgin is His Mother. Thus it was decreed from all eternity to reveal the majesty and wisdom of God.

A virgin Mother was postulated by the mission assigned to the Son of the eternal Father. As a second Adam Jesus was to undo the wrong committed by the first and become the Father of a new race. But as the first Adam was formed directly by God, so was the body of the second Adam to be formed by direct divine operation out of the flesh and blood of the virgin Mother; human generation by which the sin of Adam is transmitted from parents to child was to have no part in Him.

Thus was safeguarded the majesty of the eternal Father, who would not share the dignity of His Fatherhood with an earthly father, and would receive men again as His children only through and in His eternal Son, as the representative of all mankind and the Firstborn of all creation.

Thus, too, the place the virgin Mother would hold in the economy of man's salvation was pointed out. As Mother of the Saviour she was to become the spiritual Mother of all the redeemed and co-operate in restoring men to the supernatural order, in the loss of which the first Eve had played a fatal part. "Oh, the depth of the riches of the wisdom and of the knowledge of God! How incomprehensible are His judgments and how unsearchable His ways" (Rom. 11:13).

The Holy Spirit

Forming the Heart of Jesus in the Virgin's womb the Holy Spirit begins to act His part in the restoration of the human race. The Saviour's mission is a mission of love and the Holy Spirit is the Spirit of love. The love with which Jesus loved us to the end and shed His blood for us is the love which the Holy Spirit had enkindled in His Heart. And as the Holy Spirit unites Father and Son in His eternal love, so he must unite the redeemed with their Father and Saviour. He must transform the hearts of men into the likeness of Jesus, so that the eternal Father may recognize in them the image of His eternal Son.

A thought frequently occurring in the Epistles of St. Paul is that Christ must be formed in us, that we must have the mind of Christ, so that we may think and judge and act as Christ did, who always did the things pleasing to the Father. Such a transformation can be accomplished only through love; love is the decisive factor in man's thinking, speaking, judging, and acting, the soul of his personality. And the proof of love is action. Jesus states this plainly and unmistakably, "If anyone love me, he will keep my word. . . . He who does not love me does not keep my word" (Jn. 14:23).

Now the love of God has been poured out in our hearts by the Holy Spirit, who has been given us. Every spark of divine love in us is but a participation in the love of the Holy Spirit,

and we ought to become more fully aware of this fact. The Holy
Spirit is still too much the forgotten God. Yet it is of Him that
Jesus says, "He will glorify me, because he will take of what is
mine and declare it to you" (Jn. 16:14). The most impressive
glorification of Jesus is in the hearts of men formed after His
likeness. The Holy Spirit will do it according to our desire and
effort. Such a desire could easily be aroused and fostered by the
frequent use of the petitions addressed to the Holy Spirit in
the *Veni Sancte Spiritus:* Send us from heaven a ray of Thy
light — wash what is stained — water what is dry — heal what
is wounded, etc.

Through Mary

It is the will of God, as St. Bernard says, that all gifts of
God should reach us through Mary. The Holy Spirit has made
Mary the most perfect likeness of Christ and through her, our
spiritual Mother, He will impress this likeness upon our souls.
However, we must act as children toward Mary, not only offering
no resistance to this transformation of our hearts, but showing
our grateful appreciation by co-operating in every way. We should
beg of her to remind us of our duties, call our attention to the
inspirations of divine grace, make us understand the will of God,
lead us by the hand, support our faltering steps, lift us up when
we fall. All this does not mean anything new or unusual; it
means performing intelligently and fervently the customary de-
votional practices in honor of our heavenly Mother: the daily
Angelus, rosary, act of consecration (O my Queen, O my Mother,
I give myself entirely to thee. And to show my devotion to thee
I consecrate to thee this day my eyes, my ears, my mouth, my
whole being without reserve; keep me, guard me as thy property
and possession). Such unconditional surrender of ourselves is her
delight, that she may do in us the work she most loves to do,

that is, together with the Holy Spirit to form in us the likeness of her divine Son.

So we have received through the Holy Spirit the Heart of Jesus formed in the womb of the virgin Mother. "But to as many as received him he gave the power of becoming sons of God" (Jn. 1:12). The hope of all mankind is in Christlike Christians, in whom the Heart of Jesus has been formed by the Holy Spirit through Mary, "because all that is born of God overcomes the world" (1 Jn. 5:4).

3. HEART OF JESUS
Substantially United With the Word of God

ST. JOHN, the eagle among the Evangelists, begins his account of the life of Jesus with the words, "In the beginning was the Word and the Word was with God and the Word was God." While the other Evangelists may be said to walk with our Lord on earth, St. John soars to the heights of heaven and there shows us the person of the Saviour in the bosom of the Most Blessed Trinity. The Word of God! Though incomprehensibly profound, the term sheds a wonderful light upon our blessed Saviour, His person and His mission.

The Word of God
The term conveys the same idea as: "Image of the Father's substance," which we have already considered in the first invocation. Words are the expression of thoughts and ideas. Before words are spoken they are in the mind as purely mental words, and when they are spoken they convey to the hearer the thoughts of the speaker. What was the thought of God in the silence of eternity before creation had been called into existence? It could be nothing else but Himself. God thought of Himself and expressed this thought in a Word by which He came to know Himself. But this Word of God, giving God a perfect knowledge of Himself, cannot be merely the expression of a thought or idea as human words are. It must be equal to God in every way; it is a divine Person, possessing the same divine nature. God

24

speaking the Word is the Father, and God the eternally spoken Word is the Son.

The Hypostatic Union

This second Person of the blessed Trinity became man: "The Word became flesh and dwelt among us" (Jn. 1:14). The Word took to Himself a perfect human nature, substituting His own divine personality for the human personality which that perfect human nature would otherwise possess. This union is called the hypostatic union. It is a personal, substantial union, because the divine and human nature are united in the divine Person of the Word. The Athanasian Creed thus states the mystery of the hypostatic union, "Who (Christ), though He is God and man, is not two but one Christ. However, He is one not by a transformation of the divine into the human nature, but through the assumption of a human nature by God. He is one, not by a fusion of substances, but by the unity of the Person. For, as the rational soul and the body are but one human being, so God and man are but one Christ."

Majesty of the God-Man

Because of the hypostatic union Jesus is true God and true man. He is a divine Person and as such He must be adored in the same manner as the Father and the Holy Spirit. His human soul sees God face to face. Even as man He knows all mysteries of nature which scientists throughout the centuries have endeavored to discover, He knows all laws and forces of the universe and has complete dominion over them; i.e., He has the power of working miracles. He is not only free from sin but He is absolutely incapable of committing sin, most perfect in all His works, the model of all virtues, our Way and our Life.

Mission of the Word

Since God knows Himself in and through His eternal Word, it was fitting that the divine Word should bring the knowledge of God to men. Therefore the Word of God, Jesus Christ, speaks to men the words of God, words of truth that enlighten every man coming into the world; words of warning that men may repent and make themselves worthy of the kingdom of God; words of forgiveness that blot out the guilt of sin; words of power that drive out evil spirits and banish disease and every type of affliction; words of love that invite all those who are burdened and weary to come to Him, to find rest in His Sacred Heart; words of judgment that will assign to each and every man his place in eternity.

Because Jesus is the God-Man, He can act as our High Priest and Mediator, lifting up His voice in the assembly of the saints. Before the incarnation God was honored by created beings only; but even the most perfect worship rendered by a creature must remain limited and finite. Now the Word of God can offer to the divine majesty honor and worship of infinite value. He can offer the sacrifice of atonement that makes full and adequate reparation for the infinite offense of sin. God now can honor God through prayer, obedience, and sacrifice. This is a sublime and overwhelming mystery.

The Heart of Jesus united with the Word of God has in His exceedingly great love left His words with the Church He founded and commissioned her to make them known to the world. We are so fortunate as to know them. The all-important and decisive factor now is that we be not only hearers, but doers of the word, for, "Not everyone who says to me, 'Lord, Lord,' shall enter the kingdom of heaven; but he who does the will of my Father in heaven shall enter the kingdom of heaven" (Mt. 7:21). Loyalty and obedience to the Church in all that she teaches and commands is loyalty and obedience to Jesus. And if the powers of darkness more than ever before are at work to extinguish the light that shines in the words of Christ, and to drag men down the dark paths of sin to everlasting ruin, then so much the more tenaciously we shall cling to Him and say with St. Peter, "Lord to whom shall we go? Thou hast words of everlasting life, and we have come to believe and to know that thou art Christ, the Son of God" (Jn. 6:69).

4. HEART OF JESUS

Of Infinite Majesty

MAJESTY denotes authority, grandeur, eminence. We speak of the majesty of the law and of government; we call an extraordinarily impressive exterior a majestic appearance; the sublime expression in poetry or music is majestic. The Sacred Heart of Jesus is of infinite majesty, because there is in Jesus the infinite eminence of the Godhead and the grandeur of human nature in its highest possible exaltation. Let us look at His majesty as God and as man.

Eternal

We find no more sublime description of the majesty of the Sacred Heart of Jesus than that given us by St. John at the beginning of His Gospel, "In the beginning was the Word and the Word was with God and the Word was God." Beyond the beginning of the human race, beyond the creation of the world of angels, beyond the appearance of earth and sun and stars, beyond the beginning of any and everything that is not God stands the Word of God in the majesty of His eternity. We are impressed by age and a feeling of awe comes over us as we stand before the mighty obelisk in front of St. Peter's at Rome with its history of nearly 4000 years. We look with admiration at the ruins of the tower of Babel, at the pyramids of Egypt that speak to us of ages long past. Yet all these things had a beginning and their ruins show the effect of age; they are the silent heralds of the transitoriness of the works of man and a time

28

will come when they too will have disappeared and not a trace of them shall be left. Jesus is the Eternal One who never ages; He stands before us, not like a ruin, but in the full vigor of everlasting life.

Almighty

St. John continues, "All things were made through him, and without him was made nothing that has been made" (Jn. 1:3). In the beginning there was nothing. Now we behold around us the universe in all its vastness and glory, a world of wonders in the starry sky and endless ocean, in the countless living and lifeless creatures that cover the face of the earth. Whence are all these things? All things were made by Him. And they were made by Him not in the manner in which artists and artisans do their work, by means of materials and tools and strenuous labor, but by one word of His almighty will. The beginning of the Gospel of St. John is usually said at the end of Mass, after we have witnessed the wonders of the Eucharistic Sacrifice, immeasurably greater than the wonders of the universe. And so we kneel down at the end of the Gospel in adoration because, "We saw His glory, glory as of the only-begotten of the Father, full of grace and of truth" (Jn. 1:14). The Sacred Heart of Jesus of infinite majesty is present in the blessed Eucharist, truly, really, and substantially.

Infancy

Poor and lowly Jesus entered this world in that silent, holy night at Bethlehem; but the heavens opened and the unearthly splendor of heavenly light changed the darkness of night into the brightness of day. Angels appeared and sang a hymn, the like of which the world had never heard before, of glory to God in the highest and of peace on earth to men of good will.

He was still an Infant when wise men come from the East, led by a miraculous sign in the sky, to worship the newborn king of the Jews. Falling down before the Infant the holy Magi adored and offered their gifts of gold, frankincense, and myrrh.

Public Life

Although He appeared in the midst of men in the form of a servant, the majesty of the God-Man shone from His features, subduing, captivating, lifting up all those who were of good will.

At the beginning of His public life Jesus submitted to the baptism of penance at the hands of the Precursor. But as He stepped out of the water the heavens opened. The Holy Spirit came down upon Him in the form of a dove and a voice was heard from heaven, "This is my beloved Son, in whom I am well pleased" (Mt. 3:17).

Jesus preached the Sermon on the Mount before an immense crowd of people, and as He finished, the Evangelist tells us, "The crowds were astonished at his teaching; for he was teaching them as one having authority, and not as their scribes and Pharisees" (Mt. 7:29).

Behold Him in the boat on the storm-tossed lake. The Apostles feared that their end had come and they cried out to Him, "Lord, save us! We are perishing" (Mt. 8:26). Then He rose, commanded the wind and the sea, and "There came a great calm. And the men marveled saying, "What manner of man is this, that even the wind and the sea obey him?" (Mt. 8:27.)

The enemies of Jesus were alarmed at His rising popularity and sent the police to arrest Him. The officers of the law arrived as Jesus was teaching the people; awe-struck they listened and dared not lay hands on Him. They returned to their masters to tell them, "Never has man spoken as this man" (Jn. 7:46).

Jesus stood before the tomb of Lazarus whose body already

showed the signs of dissolution. But the power of death yielded before the majesty of the God-Man as He commanded, "Lazarus, come forth" (Jn. 11:43).

Passion

Jesus died on the cross. But in that same hour the sun veiled its face, the earth trembled, graves opened and the dead arose, the veil of the temple was rent in two. Thus nature gave testimony of the divine majesty of Him who had died, and the centurion standing by the cross confessed, "Truly he was the Son of God" (Mt. 27:54).

Resurrection

Guards were stationed at the tomb of Jesus to prevent any fraud or act of violence on the part of the disciples. Yet, as Easter morning dawned an earthquake shook the very foundation of the hill of Calvary. The stone at the entrance of the tomb was hurled aside and Jesus, the Crucified, rose from the dead in the glory of immortality. The guards themselves were the first messengers to bring the news to his enemies, who thought they had ruined Him and His work forever.

Surely, we can look into the future with serene security. What are the momentary triumphs of the forces of evil when we think of the Eternal One; what are their threats and display of power before the Almighty? The enemies of Christ come and go, their works fall to pieces and perish, but Christ conquers, His Church continues, His faithful servants pass from darkness to light, from cross to glory. This is the infinite majesty of the Sacred Heart of Jesus, the glory of the only-begotten of the Father, full of grace and of truth.

5. HEART OF JESUS
Holy Temple of God

A TEMPLE is an edifice dedicated to divine worship. We find such places of worship among all nations ancient and modern, except where, as in modern times, diabolical hatred of God and religion has done away with them. Among the temples of antiquity the one best known to Christians is the Temple of Jerusalem, sanctified by the presence of our blessed Saviour Himself. In this Temple sacrifices were offered to the true God and divine services carried on with impressive solemnity. God Himself had promised that He would fill this place with glory and listen to the prayers of those who would pray to Him. Bearing this in mind it is not hard to understand why the Sacred Heart of Jesus is called the holy temple of God. The Sacred Heart of Jesus is holy, because it is sanctified by the hypostatic union with the second Person of the most blessed Trinity. In this Heart God is present and worshiped in the most perfect manner and the most precious blessings are bestowed upon the worshiper.

Holy

The Sacred Heart of Jesus is holy, consecrated to the service of God, and the consecrator is the Holy Spirit. He came down upon the blessed Virgin and in her sanctified the material out of which this temple was to be built; He formed the Sacred Heart of Jesus in the womb of the blessed Mother and in His love united it with the Word of God. The Holy Spirit added the finishing touch to this initial consecration when at the beginning of the

32

public life of Jesus He came down upon Him in the form of a dove; and it is in the Holy Spirit that, at the end of His life, Jesus offers Himself to the Father as an immaculate victim. It was therefore a public and solemn acknowledgment of this consecration when, in the synagogue of Nazareth, Jesus applied to Himself the words of the prophet Isaias, "The Spirit of the Lord is upon me because he has anointed me; to bring good news to the poor he has sent me, to proclaim to the captives release and sight to the blind; to set at liberty the oppressed, to proclaim the acceptable year of the Lord and the day of recompense" (Lk. 4:19).

God Worshiped

The daily sacrifices and other ritual performances in the Temple of old were typical of the worship rendered to God by the Sacred Heart of Jesus during His earthly life and continued in the blessed Eucharist to the end of time.

An outer court surrounded the Temple proper and in this court stood the altar of holocausts, upon which the bloody sacrifices were offered. All these bloody sacrifices found their fulfillment in the sacrifice of our Saviour upon the cross. There the Heart of Jesus, as the divine victim, shed the last drop of blood to make atonement for the sins of the world.

The Temple proper consisted of two parts, the holy and the holy of holies. In the holy stood the altar of incense. The daily sacrifice of incense was symbolical of the prayers offered to God by His people. The sublimest prayer ever spoken on earth came from the Sacred Heart of Jesus as He entered this world, "Sacrifice and oblation thou wouldst not, but a body thou hast fitted to me. . . . Behold, I come to do thy will, O God" (Hebr. 10:5). It was the solemn closing of this prayer when Jesus cried out in His agony, "Father, if it is possible, let this cup pass away from me; yet not as I will, but as thou willest" (Mt. 26:39), and at

last, commending His soul into the hands of the Father, bowed
His head and died. Surely, this prayer ascended to the throne of
the Father with greater sweetness than the fragrance of incense.

In the holy of the Temple the altar of the loaves of proposition
was also found. These loaves were offered in thanksgiving for the
daily sustenance God provided for His people, but particularly
for the manna, with which He had fed them in the desert. The
manna and loaves of proposition were types of the bread of life,
which the Sacred Heart of Jesus provided for the chosen people
of the New Testament in Holy Communion — His own flesh
and blood.

Lastly we have the holy of holies in the Temple of old. Here
was the place for the Ark of the Covenant, which contained the
tables of the law and a vessel with manna. The Sacred Heart of
Jesus not only contains the tables of the law, but it is the Heart
of the Lawgiver Himself, and His own flesh and blood has become
the heavenly manna. Truly, the Sacred Heart of Jesus is a holy
temple.

Blessings Bestowed

When King Solomon had dedicated the Temple, the Lord
appeared to him and said, "I have chosen this place to myself as
a house of sacrifice . . . my eyes shall be open and my ears atten-
tive to the prayer of him that shall pray in this place" (2 Para.
7:12–15). These words are applied to the Sacred Heart of Jesus,
since in Him and through Him all our prayers are heard. The
Evangelists record how Jesus during His public life went about
doing good, how the people flocked to Him wherever He was
to listen to Him, to have their sins forgiven and their infirmities healed. The loving Heart of Jesus is eager to enrich all
with the abundance of His blessing. Therefore He invites all
who labor and are burdened to come to Him. He will refresh
them; with Him they shall find rest for their souls. This love of

the Sacred Heart lives on in the blessed Eucharist. Here, daily are repeated the great deeds of His power and love of which He spoke to the disciples of St. John the Baptist when He sent them back to their master to tell him that "the blind see, the lame walk, the lepers are cleansed, the deaf hear, the dead rise, the poor have the gospel preached to them" (Mt. 11:4–6). Indeed, there are millions who are spiritually blind and lame and deaf, covered with the leprosy of sin, spiritually dead. There is hope and help for all of them in the Sacred Heart of Jesus, if they but enter this holy temple of God.

Let us open our eyes and see the grandeur of the Sacred Heart of Jesus, the holy temple of God. It is open for us at all times; let us enter it. There our hunger and thirst for God shall be satisfied, there we shall find forgiveness of our sins, protection in temptation, strength in weakness, peace in tribulations. In the holy temple of Jesus' Sacred Heart all our prayers are heard and we are filled with every heavenly blessing and grace.

6. HEART OF JESUS
Tabernacle of the Most High

A TABERNACLE is a tent. During their wanderings through the desert the Israelites lived in tents. There was one tent among them distinguished above all others as the dwelling place of God. Holy Scripture speaks of it as the Tabernacle. Built by Moses according to the directions which God Himself had given, it served the people as a place of prayer and worship until they reached the promised land, where in the course of time it was replaced by the Temple. The Tabernacle gave the Israelites the comforting assurance that God was with them, that He would protect them and lead them into the land of promise. Whatever the Tabernacle meant for the Israelites the Sacred Heart of Jesus means for the Catholic Church, the chosen People of the New Testament. In this Heart God is present in our midst, protects us and leads us to heaven, the true land of promise.

God With Us

Emmanuel, God with us, is the name given to Jesus by the prophet Isaias, "Behold, a virgin shall conceive and bear a Son, and his name shall be called Emmanuel" (Isa. 7:14). God is with us in the Sacred Heart of Jesus, because it is substantially united with the Word of God and is the divine, living Tabernacle. For 33 years this living Tabernacle moved about in the midst of His people in Palestine. Then, as the Church which He had founded stepped into the place of the Old Testament's people of God, He changed His manner of presence. He established Himself as

36

the Tabernacle of the Most High in the blessed Eucharist. Thus He would remain with His people in an immeasurably more perfect manner than God was present in the Tabernacle of old. His people were to see Him, though not in human form — beneath the Eucharistic species. They were even to receive Him as the bread of life in Holy Communion. This Tabernacle of the Most High now accompanies His people on their wanderings through the desert of this world. He is with them in the grand cathedrals of our large cities as well as in the poor chapel of a lonely mission station. He accompanies them to the icy stretches of the polar regions as well as to the torrid heat of the tropics. "Neither is there any other nation so great that hath gods so nigh them, as our God is present to all our petitions" (Deut. 4:7).

Protector of His People

As the Israelites had to fight many a battle before they could take possession of the promised land, so must the chosen people of the New Dispensation fight for the heavenly land of promise. We speak of the Church as the Church Militant. But as the Tabernacle gave the Israelites the assurance of divine assistance in all dangers, so is the presence of the living Tabernacle of the Sacred Heart of Jesus the guarantee of ultimate victory for the Christian people. It is a word of comfort that Jesus leaves to His Apostles as He is about to depart from them, "Have confidence, I have overcome the world" (Jn. 16:33). This is the reason why the holy martyrs and confessors of the faith in ancient and modern times are so eager to be close to this Tabernacle of God. They want the holy Sacrifice of the Mass, even though it be offered without altar and vestments, without any solemnity of worship customary in normal times. Holy Mass brings to these valiant soldiers of Christ the body and blood of Jesus, Holy Communion, and that is the Sacred Heart of Jesus with its unconquerable love and its protection for all those who trust in Him.

As in the open warfare against the powers of hell so in the internal struggles of the soul the Tabernacle of the Most High is the protection of the faithful. When harassed by doubts, when assailed by unclean spirits, when cast down by weariness and discouragement, when groaning under the crushing weight of injustice and abandonment, we can always find consolation and strength in the Sacred Heart of Jesus. In this Tabernacle there is rest and refreshment for all those who labor and are burdened.

The Land of Promise

The wanderings of the Israelites through the desert were not to be permanent, but were to bring them to the promised land. St. Paul reminds the Christians that they have no lasting city here below but they seek the one that is to come. St. Peter tells the faithful that as strangers and pilgrims they should refrain themselves from the desires of the world. Is it not true that we so frequently experience the utter inability of the things of earth to satisfy the desires of the heart, that we long for something better, something spiritual, unchangeable, heavenly, divine?

The Israelites were led through the desert by a cloud hovering over the Tabernacle, the visible sign of the presence of God. Whenever the cloud moved, the people followed. The same divine guidance is provided for the Christian people by the Sacred Heart of Jesus. Jesus is the Light of the world, our Saviour, Leader, and King. Whosoever follows Him does not walk in darkness but has life everlasting. His words and deeds are the resplendent cloud that illuminates our way and keeps our heavenly goal before us. All the light and love of His earthly life is perpetuated in the blessed Eucharist, the memorial of all His wonderful works. We are reminded of this fact by the sanctuary lamp constantly burning before the living Tabernacle of the Most High hidden in the tabernacle of the altar.

The very thought of this Tabernacle of the Most High cannot

but keep before our eyes the nature of human life as a pilgrimage with heaven as its goal; it increases our confidence and our determination to reach the heavenly land of promise. This is precisely what St. Paul exhorts us to do, "Seek the things that are above, where Christ is seated at the right hand of God. Mind the things that are above, not the things that are on earth" (Col. 3:1 f.). And when at last the goal is reached the veil of faith shall fall, just as the walls of Jericho fell at the approach of the Israelites, and we shall behold the Tabernacle of the Most High in all its wonderful glory and live forever in its light and love.

7. HEART OF JESUS
House of God and Gate of Heaven

ON HIS flight to Mesopotamia Jacob had a remarkable dream. He saw heaven open and a ladder connecting heaven with earth. On the top of the ladder he beheld God and on the ladder itself angels were descending and ascending. At the same time Jacob heard the voice of God assuring him of protection and safe return to his native country; he would become the father of a great nation and in one of his descendants all the peoples of the earth would be blessed. When Jacob awoke he was deeply impressed and he said, "Indeed, the Lord is in this place and I knew it not. . . . How terrible is this place. This is no other than the house of God and the gate of heaven" (Gen. 28:17). And he called the name of the place Bethel, which means house of God.

The above title of the Sacred Heart of Jesus has been taken from this text of Holy Scripture. The angels ascending and descending on the ladder are God's agents in His continuous communication with men — descending with God's grace and blessing, ascending with men's prayers and good works. This heavenly business and exchange is now transacted in and through the Sacred Heart of Jesus, which can, therefore, be called in all truth a business house, a powerhouse of God's love, and the gate of heaven.

God's Business House

When Jesus remained in the Temple at the age of twelve, He explained that He must be about His Father's business. The business for which Jesus had come into the world was to save men from sin and eternal death. But business implies bilateral action, an exchange; there are two parties to it, the buyer and the seller. So it is with the business of saving souls. God offers salvation but men must pay the price. Jesus is the divine merchant. He has wonderful things to sell: truth, grace, heavenly glory. He even takes to advertising, sending out His Apostles to make His business known among all nations of the world. He teaches them how to impress upon people the value of the things they offer. These things are comparable to a treasure of immense value hidden in a field, to a pearl of such great price that the finder sells all he has in order to buy it. He dwells at length on the durability of His goods; rust and moth cannot consume them, thieves cannot steal them. At the same time He warns against imitations and impostors, false Christs, who come in the clothing of sheep, but inwardly are ravenous wolves. He wants to have branch houses established throughout the world, the Catholic churches and chapels with their priests scattered all over the globe. Surely, men must pay the price to buy His goods, and the price is good works and faithful service. But He is kind and infinitely generous. The transaction is all in favor of the buyer, and so there is a constant exchange of goods, services paid, debts canceled, fresh contracts entered. The loving Heart of Jesus is this divine business house.

God's Powerhouse

The salvation of souls calls for supernatural life and energy, a transformation of our whole being. Thoughts, intentions, deeds must be illumined and transformed by the light and life of grace. A practical illustration of what is going on in the spiritual sphere is supplied by electricity which has come to play an almost indispensable part in modern life. To obtain it not only machinery, fixtures, and bulbs are necessary, but above all the powerhouse where electricity is generated, and the power lines which conduct the current into homes and churches, schools and hospitals, offices, shops, and factories. Such a powerhouse is the Sacred Heart of Jesus generating the transforming power of love, and from it issue the power lines that conduct it into the hearts of men. There are seven main power lines, the seven sacraments. They supply the life and energy to do and to endure whatever the service of God demands, to build up, to heal and repair whatever may have become worn out or damaged. This energy is sufficient not only to save our souls but to bring us to the perfection of the saints. And Jesus not only offers this energy but He is most desirous that we should accept and use it, "I have come to cast fire upon the earth, and what will I but that it be kindled" (Lk. 12:49).

Gate of Heaven

To be saved is to enter heaven. If the Sacred Heart of Jesus supplies all the factors necessary for salvation, then It is also the gate of heaven. In fact, Jesus calls Himself the door of His sheep, "I am the door of the sheep. . . . If any one enter by me, he shall be safe . . . and shall find pastures. . . . I came that they may have life and may have it more abundantly" (Jn. 1:8–10). No one can come to the Father except through Him; no one can enter the heavenly holy of holies except in Him and through Him. He is the gate of heaven, because as our great Mediator He stands between the Father and the redeemed.

If, then, the Sacred Heart of Jesus is God's business house, let us do business there, buy the imperishable treasures of heaven with our prayers and good works, secure cancellation of our debts through His most precious blood. And if this Sacred Heart is the powerhouse of God's love, let us connect our souls with It, so that we may be able to draw from It that light and life-giving energy that will illuminate our way to heaven and supply the

necessary strength to reach it. If, finally, the Sacred Heart of
Jesus is the gate of heaven, let us abide in It by abiding in His
grace and love.

8. HEADT OF JESUS
Burning Furnace of Charity

FIRE is a symbol of love. As fire is always active, spreading, changing, consuming, so is love always active, communicating its transforming warmth and energy to others. The Sacred Heart of Jesus is said to be a burning furnace of such love. This invocation of the litany recalls the vision in which Jesus showed St. Margaret Mary His Sacred Heart surrounded by a crown of thorns and surmounted by a cross with flames issuing from the Heart and enveloping the cross. The meaning of the vision is plain. Love prompted Jesus to wear the crown of thorns and to die upon the cross. The love burning in the Sacred Heart of Jesus is the love of God and the love of men. The love of God manifests itself in Christ's love of prayer and obedience unto death; His love for men appears in His benevolence, compassion, and mercy.

Prayer

Love of God draws the soul to Him in prayer; prayer is a lifting up of the mind to God. Of the prayer life of our Saviour in His infancy nothing is recorded in holy Scripture, but it is not difficult to supply what is missing. The soul of Jesus possessed the full use of reason from the beginning of its existence and knew itself to be united to the Word of God. Is there, then, any other supposition possible but that Jesus was in uninterrupted union with His heavenly Father? Each morning found Him in prayer, praising the Father in heaven and consecrating the new day to Him; each

44

evening saw Him giving thanks for the blessings of the day.
Every created being around Him spoke to Him of His heavenly
Father: the stars in the sky, the flowers blooming in the fields,
all things living and moving over the face of the earth; all were
created by the Father through the divine Word united with His
soul. As to His prayer life during the years of His public ministry,
we have abundant information in the Gospels. He prays in the
Temple and in the synagogue, in private and in public, before
and after miracles; He spends whole nights in prayer in the soli-
tude of mountains, and He begins His Passion and closes His
life with the most sublime prayer.

Obedience

The whole life of our blessed Saviour is characterized by His
absolute and unconditional surrender to the will of His Father.
"He humbled himself, becoming obedient to death, even to death
on a cross" (Phil. 2:8). The conditions of His life called for the
heroic practice of obedience. The poverty of Bethlehem, the
flight into Egypt, the hidden years at Nazareth are unintelligible
from the human point of view; however, they were the will of
the Father and Jesus delighted in submitting. So it continued
during His public life. Jesus endured hardships and privations,
contempt and opposition, ingratitude, and in the end the cross
with all its pain and shame. Yet, Jesus had come to do His
Father's will. He entered the world with an act of submission upon
His lips, "Sacrifice and oblation thou wouldst not, but a body
thou hast fitted to me. . . . Behold, I come . . . to do thy will, O
God" (Hebr. 10:7). To do His Father's will was His daily meat
and to have accomplished the task assigned to Him by the
Father was His joy and satisfaction at the end of His life. Thus
He prayed on the eve of His Passion, "I have glorified thee on
earth; I have accomplished the work which thou hast given me
to do" (Jn. 17:4).

Benevolence

All labors and suffering undergone by Jesus for the honor of the Father were also means to save souls. Jesus loved men, because He saw them as children of His heavenly Father. This love shone from His face in that kind benevolence that attracted crowds of people to Him wherever He went. He journeyed about the country teaching and doing good to all. No class of people was excluded from His love. He loved the little children, called them to Himself and blessed them; He healed the sick and consoled the sorrowing. He had compassion on the poor widow of Naim and raised her son to life; He felt the grief of Mary and Martha over the death of Lazarus and brought joy to their hearts by raising their brother from the dead. He invited all who labor and are burdened to come to Him; He would refresh them and with Him they would find rest for their souls.

Mercy

There was one class of people, that claimed the special love of our Saviour's Heart; they were the poorest of the poor, the sinners. For them He was the Good Shepherd that sought the lost sheep and rejoiced when He had found it; for them He was the physician that had come to heal. The Pharisees in their hypocritical righteousness were scandalized and said, "He goes with sinners and eats with them" (Mk. 3:16). They had no idea of the intensity of the love that burned in the furnace of His loving Heart. He continued to be the Friend of sinners in spite of their criticism and condemnation. He forgave the woman guilty of adultery, He allowed Himself to be anointed by Mary Magdalen, the sinful woman; He cast a look of merciful love upon Peter who had shamefully denied Him, and offered forgiveness even to His traitor. As He hung upon the cross, excruciating pain burning in His body and agony raging in His soul, He prayed for His enemies, promised paradise to the repentant thief, and bequeathed to us the most precious treasure which He still possessed, His holy Mother. He died and allowed His Heart to be pierced so that we might be able to look into the depths of this burning furnace of charity.

We too have been and daily are the recipients of Jesus' burning love. Through the love of His Heart we were cleansed from sin and transformed into children of God, and now we enjoy the abundance of the blessings of the Catholic Church. Is it too much for us to love Him in return and our fellow men for His sake? There is so little love in the world. Because iniquity abounds, charity has grown cold and the icy blasts of hatred make men shiver and fear. The task of the Christian is to draw men to the Sacred Heart of Jesus through deeds of love. Wars will disappear, justice and peace will flourish, when men are welded together by the charity burning in our Saviour's loving Heart.

9. HEART OF JESUS
Abode of Justice and Love

THE word abode in this invocation of the litany is the translation of the Latin word *receptaculum,* which means receptacle, that is, a vessel or a place in which something is deposited or kept. The Sacred Heart of Jesus is the receptacle of justice and love, not only in the sense that Jesus possessed these virtues in the highest possible degree, but also in the sense that through this Heart God manifested His justice and love in the most striking manner. Jesus endured the full rigor of divine justice in atoning for sin; He suffered for the pride of sin in His humiliations, for the pleasure of sin in excruciating pain of soul and body. At the same time Jesus was the object of the Father's most tender love and the instrument through which God bestowed His gifts of love upon men.

Pride Atoned by Humiliation

Pride is self-exaltation to the extent of refusing submission to the authority of God. God says, "The Lord thy God thou shalt worship and him only shalt thou serve" (Mt. 4:10), and the sinner says, "I will not serve." This is the sin of Lucifer and the sin of our first parents; it is implied with various degrees of malice in every sin. Jesus took the punishment of this pride upon Himself in the humiliations of His life and especially His Passion. He, the Son of the eternal Father, took the form of a servant, becoming obedient to death, even to death upon a cross. He became like unto us in all things, sin alone excepted. We behold the climax of this humiliation in the Passion. There the justice of God struck the blow with relentless rigor. "Despised and the most abject of men, a man of sorrow and afflicted with infirmity. . . . And we have thought him as it were a leper and as one struck by God and afflicted" (Isa. 54:3 f.). The royal prophet puts these words upon the lips of the Saviour as He hangs upon the cross in shame and disgrace, "I am a worm and no man, the reproach of men and the outcast of the people. All they that saw me laughed me to scorn" (Ps. 21:7 f.).

Pleasure Atoned by Pain

There is a certain pleasure in every sin, and it is for the sake of this pleasure that sin is committed. It is expressly mentioned in connection with the first sin ever committed: "Eve saw that the tree was good to eat and fair to the eyes and delightful to behold" (Gen. 3:6). The pleasures of the palate are before the glutton and the drunkard, the thrill of the flesh subdues the impure, the love of comfort and ease makes the slothful deaf to the calls of duty. The proper punishment of sinful pleasure is pain. Therefore Jesus suffered what no man ever suffered or could suffer. The sorrowful mysteries of the rosary recall the principal features of His Passion; the crucifix tells the final chapter of the justice that struck the Sacred Heart of Jesus.

Honor for Humiliation

The Sacred Heart of Jesus that endured the rigors of divine justice is also the receptacle of the Father's most tender love. Twice during His public life, at the baptism and the transfiguration of Jesus, the voice of the Father was heard, "This is my beloved Son, in whom I am well pleased" (Mt. 3:17). The same Apostle who speaks so impressively of the humiliation of Jesus in His life also adds, "Therefore also God has exalted him and has bestowed upon him a name that is above every name, so that in

the name of Jesus every knee should bend of those in heaven, on
earth and under the earth and every tongue should confess that
the Lord Jesus Christ is in the glory of God the Father" (Phil.
2:9 ff.). What a glorification of Jesus, when He gloriously came
forth from the tomb and ascended into heaven; what will it be
when He shall return on the last day on the clouds of heaven
with great power and majesty to judge the living and the dead.
All power is given to Him in heaven and on earth. His word is
the law of the world; His sentence will fix the destinies of men
for all eternity and of His kingdom there shall be no end.

Delight for Pain

For the pain Jesus endured in atoning for sin the Father
bestowed upon Him the delights of His love. In the midst of all
His sufferings the Sacred Heart of Jesus enjoyed the beatific
vision of God and His soul rejoiced in the Holy Spirit; sweet
and imperturbable peace dwelt in Him. His Resurrection was the
beginning of glorious immortality and impassibility even for His
body. It shone like the sun and moved with the speed of spirits,
doors and walls offering no obstacle. "Christ having risen from
the dead dies now no more, death shall no longer have dominion
over him" (Rom. 6:9). The consummation of the delights of the
Sacred Heart of Jesus however will come when at the Last Judgment He will be able to call to the possession of the heavenly
kingdom all those who were saved through the humiliations and
sufferings of His Passion. Their everlasting glory and joy is the
sweetest delight of His loving Heart. Indeed, it is for this union
with His redeemed that He prayed on the very eve of His
Passion, "Father I will that where I am they also whom thou
hast given me may be with me, in order that they may behold
my glory. . . . That the love with which thou hast loved me may
be in them and I in them" (Jn. 17:24 ff.).

The Heart of Jesus as the abode of justice reminds us of

the malice of sin, for God could not have punished sin more than it deserves. The thought of this malice must strengthen us to combat the pride of sin through humble obedience and submission to God's will in all conditions of life, and to atone for sinful pleasure by works of penance. On the other hand, the Heart of Jesus as the abode of love keeps us mindful of the infinite goodness of God and draws us to imitate the Sacred Heart of Jesus in His humility, obedience, and patient suffering. As with Jesus, so with us, humiliations and sufferings willingly endured in atonement of sin will be rewarded by peace of soul such as the world cannot give, and in the end by the delights of our glorious resurrection and life everlasting.

10. HEART OF JESUS
Full of Goodness and Love

ON A certain occasion a rich young man approached Jesus and kneeling before Him said, "Good Master, what shall I do to gain eternal life?" At first hearing, the answer of Jesus appears startling, "Why do you call me good? No one is good but God only." This young man apparently took Jesus for more than an ordinary teacher; by calling Him good he did not mean to say that Jesus was merely kind and wise, but good in a fuller sense of the word, i.e., perfect in His relation to God. From Him therefore he wishes to learn how to be good, to do good in order to gain eternal life. Jesus wants to reward the good will of this young man and to lead him to a clearer knowledge of Himself. There is only one who is really, totally, and essentially good, and that is God. To say that God is good is to say that He is infinitely perfect in His being and in His work. If Jesus is good in that sense, then He is God. The young man may not have this clear knowledge of Jesus as yet, but keeping the commandments and accepting the invitation to follow Jesus will in due time lead him to that knowledge. But this young man was too much attached to his riches and did not accept the call of Jesus.

We, who believe in Jesus as our God and Saviour, know that He is infinitely good and perfect, the source of all that makes us good and perfect, pleasing to God, deserving of eternal life. And being full of love and seeking our best, He makes us sharers in His goodness. In the hymn for the Lauds of the Feast of Corpus

Christi St. Thomas has admirably described this goodness of Jesus, for he tells us that Jesus has given Himself in birth as our companion, at the Last Supper as our food, on the cross as our ransom, and in heaven as our reward.

Our Companion

The prophet Isaias speaks of the Messias as Emmanuel, which means, God with us. What was it that prompted the Son of the eternal Father to assume the nature of man, a nature subject to the shortcomings of matter, to hunger and thirst, heat and cold, sensitive to ingratitude, humiliation and fear? He did it because He loved us and saw that it was good for us. The human heart by its very nature longs to be close to God. It was the deception of the ancient serpent that led man to abandon God; once separated from Him, man could not of his own power regain the companionship of God that he had enjoyed in Paradise. But God had not ceased to love man and so He sent His only-begotten Son into the world to be our companion, "And the Word was made flesh and dwelt among us" (Jn. 1:14). God is now with men. Jesus is born at Bethlehem, grows up among men, associates with them, teaches them, listens to their tales of sorrow, helps in their sufferings, forgives their sins. Being full of goodness and of love He spends Himself to make men happy by sharing in His goodness. So He had spoken as the divine Wisdom even before His incarnation, "My delights were to be with the children of men" (Prov. 8:31).

Our Food

The loving Heart of Jesus wants to share His goodness with us not only through His presence and work, but through a wonderful and mystical communication of His whole Self, and He wants to do this for all future generations. He makes Himself their spiritual food and drink. This is what He said in the syna-

gogue of Capharnaum, "The bread that I will give is my flesh
for the life of the world. . . . He who eats my flesh and drinks
my blood has life everlasting, and I will raise him up on the
last day" (Jn. 6:52 ff.). At the Last Supper He made this promise
a reality. Then and there, on the eve of His sacred Passion, He
took bread, blessed and broke it and gave it to His disciples
and said, "Take this and eat; this is my body." And taking a
cup, He gave thanks and gave it to them saying, "All you drink
of this; for this is my blood . . ." (Mt. 26:26 f.). This is more
than teaching and working miracles and forgiving sins. It is the
most thorough and intimate penetration of our whole being with
the life and energy of the God-Man. What could be a greater
good for us? The love of the Sacred Heart has given it.

Our Ransom

Holy Church sings of this gift of the Sacred Heart in the
Exultet on Holy Saturday: "O wondrous condescension of Thy
kindness toward us; O tenderness of love surpassing understanding,
that to ransom a slave Thou didst give up the Son. O sin of
Adam truly necessary, to be blotted out by the death of Christ.
O happy guilt that merited to have a Redeemer so great and so
good." To enjoy the pleasure of sin man had paid the price of
his life and liberty, making himself the slave of satan, and there
was nothing left to him by which he could have redeemed himself. The love of God took pity on him. The Son of God took
our sins upon Himself and paid the ransom when He died upon
the cross. According to St. Paul, Jesus nailed the note of our
indebtedness to the cross. His life was overflowing, superabundant
ransom, by which the price was paid not only for our liberty,
but also for all the other graces and blessings which so wonderfully enrich the Christian life. Redemption is a good of infinite
value, and we should never forget to whom we owe it: "You
know that you were redeemed . . . not with silver or gold, but

with the precious blood of Christ, as of a lamb without blemish and without spot" (1 Pet. 1:19).

Our Reward

Having loved us to the end, to the shedding of the last drop of His blood, Jesus cannot forget us in heaven. On the eve of His death He tells His Apostles that in His Father's house there are many mansions and that He is going to prepare a place for them. In His high priestly prayer He addresses the last petition to His heavenly Father on behalf of His own: "Father, I will that where I am, they also whom thou hast given me may be with me; in order that they may behold my glory. . . . In order that the love with which thou hast loved me, may be in them, and I in them" (Jn. 17:24 ff.). In His glory He is the highest good of all the blessed in heaven, for heavenly beatitude is fundamentally and essentially the vision of God face to face, and Jesus is God. This is the climax of the goodness and unselfish love of our Saviour's Sacred Heart: to reward us for having accepted His grace and blessing, for having done the things that are for our peace and having followed Him to victory in the conflicts of life. For doing good to ourselves by the gifts of His bounty He gives Himself to be our everlasting reward.

We now understand better why Jesus is the good Master, and why He calls the attention of the rich young man to the fact that God alone is good. The Heart of Jesus is full of goodness and love because it is the Heart of God. All that makes us good in this life, worthy of the name of Christian, fit for life eternal, is His gift. But the crown of all His gifts, the energizing power active in His gifts, is Himself: He is our companion on our way to heaven, our food for our life, our ransom as our Brother, our reward as our beatitude everlasting. He is the highest good; to possess Him is to possess all that is good, to lose Him is to lose all that is good. O Heart of Jesus, full of goodness and love!

11. HEART OF JESUS
Abyss of All Virtues

WE THINK of an abyss as an immeasurable depth. We use the word frequently in a figurative sense, of good as well as of evil. Thus we speak of an abyss of love, of goodness, but also of an abyss of malice, of vice. The goodness or malice in either case is so great that we cannot fathom it. In calling the Sacred Heart of Jesus an abyss of all virtues we wish to say that He possesses all virtues in such perfection that we cannot grasp their grandeur nor sound their depth. There is no virtue, no matter how difficult to practice and how rare among men, that is not found in Him, none that is not present in Him in all its possible perfection, without flaw or deficiency.

Christian Perfection

Christian perfection calls for the presence of all virtues. However, it is possible that the one or other virtue may be weak and deficient, or that, because of such deficiency, virtue coexists with faults and even sin. A man may be pious but at the same time proud and domineering, charitable but also impatient and intolerant, temperate but still narrow and greedy, just while he is harsh and unforgiving. Even among the saints, we find heroic sanctity along with human faults and shortcomings. Virtues may also be present in various degrees of perfection. Frequently saints distinguish themselves in the practice of one particular virtue. Thus, St. Paul was distinguished by indomitable zeal in his missionary labors, St. Francis of Assisi by love of poverty,

St. Francis de Sales by meekness, St. Aloysius by contempt of the world, St. Theresa of the Child Jesus by childlike simplicity. But all saints could have been more perfect even in the virtue in which they excelled, and one saint may be more perfect than another. Our blessed Mother certainly possessed all virtues in a higher degree than all saints put together.

Perfection of Christ

In Jesus we behold a wonderful harmonious blending of all virtues. His virtues are without flaw or deficiency, in a degree of perfection that cannot be increased, because in Him virtue shares in the unfathomable depth and infinity of the Godhead. In Him there is love without selfishness, obedience without servility, patience without weakness, firmness without pride, courage without recklessness, authority without haughtiness.

Absorbed in the presence of God whom He beholds face to face, He is yet most active in behalf of men, whether it be in the carpenter shop at Nazareth doing manual work, or following the highways and byways of Palestine in quest of the lost sheep, preaching to the multitudes, healing their sick, driving out devils, consoling the sorrowing. Obedient unto death and respecting authority, He is fearless in denouncing vice. Though full of kindness and mercy toward the sinner, He is unyielding toward sin. Having healed the man who had been sick for 38 years He dismisses him with the warning, "Behold, thou art cured; sin no more, lest something worse befall thee" (Jn. 5:14). Harmony of love and firmness shines forth in the relation of Jesus to His Apostles. He had chosen them to be the pillars of His Church and He loved them. Yet even in their regard He insists upon His unchangeable rights as God-Man. It was at the Last Supper, when Jesus had instituted the blessed Eucharist and celebrated the first holy Mass, had made the Apostles the first priests and bishops of the New Testament and had given Himself to them in Holy Communion, that He addressed to them the awe-inspiring words, "You are my friends, if you do the things I command you. . . . You have not chosen me, but I have chosen you" (Jn. 15:15 f.). Notwithstanding their election and the privileges bestowed upon them, His friendship with them comes to an end the moment they refuse to do what He commands. This is the most perfect harmony of virtues, governed by the unchanging principles of justice and love.

Jesus and the Saints

Thus above all the saints, Mary the Queen of all angels and saints not excepted, stands Jesus in the unapproachable majesty and holiness of His Sacred Heart. Compared to His holiness the virtues of all saints disappear. Just as the beauty of the starry sky becomes invisible at the rising of the sun, so does the holiness of the saints disappear in the presence of the divine Sun of justice. And just as the light of the moon is but the reflection of the light of the sun, so are the virtues of the saints nothing but a faint reflection of the virtues of the Sacred Heart of Jesus. Whatever virtue and holiness is found in them has its origin in but is infinitely surpassed by the holiness of the Sacred Heart of Jesus, the abyss of all virtues.

Called to Imitation

Although the perfection of the Sacred Heart of Jesus is beyond our reach, Jesus calls upon us to imitate His example: "I have given you an example, that as I have done to you, so you also should do" (Jn. 13:15). Not equality but similarity is possible. In particular Jesus calls our attention to two of His virtues: "Learn from me, for I am meek and humble of heart; and you will find rest for your souls" (Mt. 11:29). Humility is the foundation of Christian perfection. The humble man is conscious of his nothingness and his need of God's mercy; therefore he submits to God's holy will and prays for and relies upon the grace of God. The prayer of the humble pierces the clouds and God will exalt him. Therefore St. Augustine lays down as a principle for the Christian who strives after perfection, first of all to lay the foundation of humility.

Out of humility grows meekness. Meekness controls our temper, prevents the outbursts of anger and impatience, enables us to bear with the faults and failings of others, even to suffer their injustices without resentment or revenge. For the preservation of peace among men there is probably no other virtue of greater importance. Meekness fosters charity and charity is the fulfillment of the whole law. In an atmosphere of peace and charity all other virtues will flourish and bring forth the most beautiful fruits of holiness.

Jesus, meek and humble of heart, make our hearts like unto Thine.

12. HEART OF JESUS
Most Worthy of All Praise

WE PRAISE a beautiful piece of art, a noble deed, a good intention, the excellence of a man's character. The Sacred Heart of Jesus is most worthy of all praise, because every excellence of nature and grace, of character and work is found in Him. In connection with the above invocation we wish to consider the divinity of Jesus and His work as the basis of the praise due to Him; these reflections will in their turn suggest the practical form in which such praise should be rendered.

The Heart of God

Jesus is the Son of the eternal Father and substantially united with the Word of God, equal to the Father in perfection and glory. The words of the psalmist therefore apply also to Him, "Great is the Lord and greatly to be praised, and of his greatness there is no end" (Ps. 47:2). Jesus is eternal; before Abraham was made He is. He is the Word of God that was in the beginning, and all things that were made were made by Him. It is He, therefore, through whom all things were made according to number, measure, and weight. He is infinitely wise and together with the Father and the Holy Spirit governs the world with such providence that not even a sparrow falls from the roof without His will. Jesus is the Holy One seen by Daniel in prophetic vision and as the Holy One He is announced to the Blessed Virgin by the archangel Gabriel. Not even His most bitter enemies can accuse Him of sin, because He always does the things pleasing to the Father.

If the saints are deserving of praise because of their heavenly wisdom and holiness of life, then the Sacred Heart of Jesus, the Holy One and abyss of all virtues, is most worthy of all praise. "Thine, O Lord, is magnificence and power and glory and victory and to thee is praise; for all that is in heaven and on earth is thine . . . in thy hands are greatness and the empire of all things" (1 Para. 29:11–13).

The Heart of the Saviour

When Jesus made His solemn entry into Jerusalem, crowds of people gathered around Him, broke branches from the trees and scattered them on the road, spread their garments before Him, and rent the air with their shouts of joy and jubilation: "Hosanna to the Son of David! Blessed is he who comes in the name of the Lord" (Mt. 21:9). We hear the same words in every holy Mass as the Church prepares for His coming upon the altar for the unbloody offering of the sacrifice of our salvation. Blessed, indeed, is Jesus by the Father and the Holy Spirit, for never was a work undertaken that brought greater glory to God than the saving mission of the Redeemer of the world. Blessed is He by the saints in heaven, for all their holiness is due to Him, to His grace and the inspiration of His life. Blessed is He by the just on earth, for He is their strength and their hope of salvation. Blessed is He, because He is our Saviour. He has saved us from the slavery of satan. He has brought good news to the poor; He has proclaimed release to the captives and sight to the blind, set at liberty the oppressed, enriched us with heavenly blessings and made us heirs of heaven. He has announced the day of recompense when we shall hear the appraisal of our work from the lips of our divine Judge, "Well done, good and faithful servant . . . enter into the joy of thy Master" (Mt. 25:21). Is not the Saviour's Sacred Heart deserving of all our praise? And how shall we praise Him?

Prayer and Imitation

For all too many people prayer means only petition for material blessings. The greatness and glory of the God-Man and His right to praise and thanksgiving escape their attention; at least it finds no place in their private devotion. Let us lift up our minds and hearts to contemplate the majesty of the God-Man, the ardor and unselfishness of His love, and we shall spontaneously break into prayer of praise, "We praise Thee, we bless Thee, we give Thee thanks." What we praise we shall seek to acquire if it is within our reach, and imitation of the Sacred Heart of Jesus is within our power. In fact, Jesus calls for it. We are to learn from Him as He is meek and humble of heart; we are to do as He has done. The Apostle assures us, "This is the will of God, your sanctification" (1 Thess. 4:3). The imitation of the Sacred Heart of Jesus is practical praise and exceeds in excellence any praise of words.

Zeal for Souls

The praise of the Sacred Heart by imitation also will prompt us to join Him in His work of saving souls in order that He may be glorified the more. Jesus wants to save men through men; He wants our co-operation. The desire of His Sacred Heart for our co-operation is expressed in His words, "The harvest is abundant, but the laborers are few; pray therefore the Lord of the harvest to send forth laborers into his harvest" (Lk. 10:2). Before His eyes stood those millions of souls ripe for the grace of salvation and waiting for someone to bring to them the message of the Gospel. The same desire prompts the last command He gives to the Apostles before He ascended into heaven, "Go, therefore, and make disciples of all nations, baptizing them in the name of the Father and of the Son and of the Holy Spirit, teaching them to observe all that I have commanded you" (Mt. 28:20).

A vast field of action is open for fulfilling our desire to praise the Sacred Heart of Jesus. We can pray for the extension of Christ's kingdom on earth, implore by acts of faith, hope, charity, patience in suffering, and mortification the grace of faith and conversion for pagans and sinners; we can support the mission work of the Church in a material way; we can foster priestly, religious, and missionary vocations. We shall then consider ourselves privileged to have a member of the family in the army of Christ's Apostles and gratefully accept the call to such work, should God extend it to us personally.

To give praise to the Sacred Heart of Jesus is the glorious task assigned to us as members of His Church. Let us dedicate ourselves to it with renewed fervor and love, so that soon the one cry, "Praise to the divine Heart that wrought our salvation; to It be honor and glory forever," may resound throughout the earth.

13. HEART OF JESUS
King and Center of All Hearts

IN THE jubilee year of 1925 Pope Pius XI issued an encyclical on Christ the King and established the feast. "That Christ should be styled king in the figurative meaning of the word has long been of common usage," he wrote, "on account of the exalted excellence by which He eminently surpasses all created things. Thus it happens that He is said to reign in the minds of men, not so much because of mental power or great extent of knowledge as because He is the very truth, and mortal man must necessarily derive and obediently accept from Him the truth. He reigns likewise in the wills of men, because in Him there is an altogether perfect integrity and compliance of the human will with the holiness of the divine will, and He so subjects our free will by His own influence and impulse as to make us aspire to all that is most noble. Christ, finally, is acknowledged as King of hearts on account of His charity, surpassing all knowledge, and a meekness and benignity attracting souls." These words of the encyclical give us a brief commentary on the present invocation of the Sacred Heart of Jesus as King and Center of all hearts.

Prophecies

The Old as well as the New Testament speaks of Christ as King in the most exalted and comprehensive meaning of the term. He is the Ruler that will come out of Jacob and is constituted by the Father King over His holy Mount of Sion, who will receive the nations as His inheritance and the ends of the earth for His possession. He is the Prince of peace and government is laid upon His shoulders. His empire shall be multiplied and there shall be no end of peace. The first announcement of Him in the New Testament dwells on the greatness of His kingship. Gabriel, the archangel, informs the Blessed Virgin, chosen to be the Mother of the Messias, that, "The Lord God will give him the throne of David his father, and he shall be King over the house of Jacob forever; and of his kingdom there shall be no end" (Lk. 1:32 f.).

Before Pilate

Jesus speaks of Himself as King only once. It is the morning of the first Good Friday. Jesus stands before Pilate. Jesus, weak and exhausted from what He has suffered during the terrible night, manacled, with the smirch of spittle on His face, stands before Pilate, the King of kings before the representative of the Roman emperor, the Creator before the creature, the Holiest of the holy before a cowardly judge. It is under such circumstances that Pilate asks the question, "Art thou the king of the Jews?" A solemn question, and Jesus gives a solemn answer, "My kingdom is not of this world. . . . My kingdom is not from hence."

Pilate therefore said to Him, "Thou art then a king?" Jesus answered, "Thou sayest it; I am a King. This is why I was born and why I have come into the world, to bear witness to the truth . . ." (Jn. 18:33 ff.). The kingdom of Christ is a spiritual kingdom; He rules over the minds and hearts of men as supreme teacher, lawgiver, and judge.

The King

Jesus is King of truth. We have a summary of His teaching in the Sermon on the Mount. Blessed are the poor in spirit, the meek, the sorrowful, they that hunger and thirst after justice, the merciful, the pure of heart, the peacemakers, those who suffer persecution for the sake of justice. We could not imagine a sharper contrast between the principles enunciated by Jesus and those of the world. But they are true and Jesus has come to give testimony to the truth.

Jesus' kingdom is the kingdom of holiness. The idea of Christ's kingdom is not external appearance, not lip service, but the perfection of a sincere heart. Men are to be perfect as their Father in heaven is perfect. God sees their innermost thoughts and intentions and these are decisive for the goodness of the external act. God must be loved with the whole heart, the whole mind, the whole soul, and all our strength. His followers must always bear in mind that the way of salvation is the close way with the narrow gate. The broad way to which the world invites leads to ruin, temporal and eternal.

Jesus is Judge. The Father has given all judgment to the Son. In the full consciousness of His divine kingship Jesus describes His coming for judgment. He will come in the clouds of heaven with great power and majesty. All nations shall be gathered before Him and He will pronounce the sentence of eternal salvation or damnation. And then His heavenly kingdom in all its glory will begin.

Center of All Hearts

The heart of man has been made for God and only in and through the Heart of Jesus can men find Him. The goodness of God has appeared in visible form in Jesus. During His earthly life the charm of His love attracted the people with irresistible force, so that they followed Him wherever He went. He went about doing good. In the same manner He continues to attract souls and to do good in the blessed Eucharist, the memorial of His love. From every tabernacle, from every consecrated host issues the invitation to all who labor and are heavily burdened to come to Him. He will refresh them and with Him they will find rest for their souls. But love kindles love, and so we behold the wonderful spectacle of millions of men and women loving Jesus as they love no other man, ready to shed for Him the last drop of their blood. No man was ever loved as Jesus is loved. The great heroes of nations may be loved by their countrymen during life, they may be honorably mentioned in books of history, monuments may have been built in their honor, but who of them could be said to be loved centuries after his death? To be loved a man must be present, must live. Jesus lives. He lives in the Eucharist, He lives in the Church, He lives in the hearts of men. And it is living, personal love that speaks when the faithful consecrate themselves again and again to the Sacred Heart of Jesus, "Thine we are and Thine we wish to be."

The more men love Jesus, the closer they approach His Sacred Heart as the center of their love, the more they will love one another; they come closer to one another just as lines drawn from the periphery of a circle come closer to one another the closer they approach the center. Therefore the hope of mankind lies in the Sacred Heart of Jesus. Let men gather around the Heart of their King and the love and peace of His kingdom will descend upon this troubled world.

14. HEART OF JESUS
In Whom Are All the Treasures of Wisdom and Knowledge

WISDOM is the ability to choose the best means for the attainment of a given end. The most important and all-decisive end of life is God, the blessed vision of whom is eternal beatitude. Therefore the highest type of wisdom is to make all earthly things serve for the attainment of this end. Knowledge is the possession of truth. The most important truth for us to know is that we are on earth to know, love, and serve God and thus to save our souls. Hence the author of the *Imitation of Christ* can say, "This is the highest wisdom: through contempt of the world to strive after the kingdom of heaven" (Im. Ch., I, 1). Such wisdom and knowledge are treasures of inestimable value and they are found in all their fullness and perfection in the Sacred Heart of Jesus. "And the Spirit of the Lord shall rest upon Him; the Spirit of wisdom; . . . the Spirit of knowledge and godliness" (Isa. 11:2).

Wisdom at Work
Wisdom seeks God in all things and rejoices in doing the things that please Him. The very first act of Jesus' soul was an act of wisdom, an expression of His readiness to do His Father's will: "Sacrifice and oblation thou wouldst not, but a body thou hast fitted to me. . . . Behold, I come . . . to do thy will, O God" (Hebr. 10:5 ff.). When He was born at Bethlehem angels announced the program of His life: "Glory to God in the highest,

68

and peace on earth among men of good will" (Lk. 2:14). As a boy of twelve He remained in the Temple, even without the knowledge of Mary and Joseph, because He must be about His Father's business. When in holy indignation He drove out of the Temple buyers and sellers, the Apostles remembered that it had been written of Him, "The zeal for thy house has eaten me up" (Jn. 2:17). Jesus assured His hearers that in His teaching as well as in His miracles He did not seek His own glory but the glory of the Father. In His high priestly prayer He summed up His life's work by saying that He had glorified the Father. To glorify the Father He became obedient unto death, even death on a cross. And as the priest and victim of the Eucharistic sacrifice He will glorify the Father to the end of the world. The clean oblation is offered from the rising of the sun to the going down thereof, and the name of God is great among the gentiles. There could be no more perfect subordination of a whole life to one leading idea than what we behold in the life of Jesus. Everything from the beginning to the end is subordinated to the glory of the Father, and that is wisdom. All the treasures of wisdom are found in His Sacred Heart.

Knowledge Assisting Wisdom

True knowledge makes us see in all created things means to glorify God and to save our souls. Thus knowledge stands in the service of wisdom. The value of created things lies in the help which they offer toward the attainment of this end; for the rest they are worthless. They may even become a danger and obstacle to salvation. Such true knowledge fills the Sacred Heart of Jesus.

Nature Speaks of God

For Jesus all the things of nature are souvenirs of His Father. He sees the lilies of the fields clothed by the Father more beau-

tifully than Solomon arrayed in all his glory. The birds of the
air are fed by the Father and not one of them falls to the
ground without His will. It is the Father who lets the sun shine
upon the good and the evil and gives rain to all in due season.
If God thus takes care of irrational creatures, how much more
will He take care of men who are His children. Let them cast
all their cares upon their Father in heaven. One thing only
they must attend to and that is to seek God and His justice
and all things needful for their lives shall be added unto them.

A Necessity

But to us in our fallen state, the good things of this earth
can become a danger to salvation. In enjoying these things we
are liable to forget the Giver and the purpose for which the
things were given. A very determined attitude, therefore, is de-
manded by our Lord in such circumstances. Even an eye must
be plucked out, a hand or a foot cut off, if they are an obstacle
to salvation. For what does it profit a man if he gain the whole
world but suffer the loss of his soul?

Example of Jesus

Jesus illustrates His teaching by His example and thus proves
Himself in the possession of perfect knowledge. Though divinely
rich He became poor; though all honor is due to Him He
humbled Himself taking the form of a servant. Though all
power is given to Him in heaven and on earth, He becomes a
helpless babe, and for the years of His hidden life He is subject
to Mary and Joseph. In His public life He prefers hardships and
privations to the comforts of wealth and shows no regard for
the opinion of men. Having set joy before Him He chose the
sorrows and disgrace of the cross, because they served the glory
of His Father more effectively. Thus Jesus exemplifies the work
of knowledge. He loves and uses earthly things where they direct

the mind to God and are helpful in giving honor to the Father; for the rest they are worthless to Him.

Wisdom and knowledge are of incalculable value and all their treasures are found in the Sacred Heart of Jesus. We can and must make them our own through prayer and reflection on the words and the example of our Blessed Saviour. They will be for us a source of fervor, contentment, and strength in adversities. Holy Church puts a beautiful prayer for such wisdom and knowledge on our lips in the Postcommunion of the feast of the Sacred Heart: "May Thy sacred mysteries, O Lord Jesus, give us a holy fervor, so that perceiving the sweetness of Thy most loving Heart, we may learn to despise earthly things and to love those of heaven."

15. HEART OF JESUS
In Whom Dwells the Fullness of Divinity

THE divinity of Christ has been and is still denied by millions of men. The idea of a God in human form is relegated to the realm of fairy tales and poetic fiction. At the same time many of those who deny the divinity of Christ would make Him the greatest teacher and social reformer the world has ever seen; they say His own claim to be the Son of God is due to some mental complex for which He cannot be made responsible. It escapes their attention that one who suffers from mental aberrations cannot be a reliable leader in the field of morality or social reform. Proofs for the divinity of Christ are contained in most of the invocations of the Litany of the Sacred Heart as we consider them. Here we wish to confine ourselves to the testimony which Christ gives of Himself and draw from it some conclusions as to the significance of Christ for the world.

Equal to the Father

Jesus claimed to have the same nature as the Father when He said, "I and the Father are one" (Jn. 10:30). He attributed eternity to Himself when He told the Jews that "Before Abraham came to be, I am" (Jn. 8:58). In both cases the Jews wanted to stone Him, because they considered Him guilty of blasphemy, thus showing that they understood Him to mean exactly what He said. His power and authority are equal to that of the Father, "For whatever he does, this the Son also does in like manner. . . . As the Father raises the dead and gives them life, even so the

72

Son also gives life to whom he will . . . that all may honor the Son even as they honor the Father. . . . As the Father has life in himself, even so he has given to the Son also to have life in himself" (Jn. 5:19 ff.).

Forgiving Sins

When Jesus was about to heal a certain paralytic, He first said to him, "Son, thy sins are forgiven thee." At once the Jews accused Him of blasphemy, for God alone can forgive sins. Thereupon Jesus asked the question, "Which is easier, to say to the paralytic, Thy sins are forgiven thee, or to say, Arise, and take up thy pallet, and walk?" Of course, neither of these is easier, for both call for the exercise of divine power. And so Jesus continued, "But that you may know that the Son of man has power on earth to forgive sins . . . I say to thee, arise, take up thy pallet and go to thy house" (Mk. 2:4 ff.). And immediately the health of the sick man was restored.

Profession of St. Peter

Since many of the people took Jesus for one of the great prophets, He asked the Apostles on a certain occasion whom *they* thought Him to be. Then Peter, in the name of the other Apostles, made this solemn declaration, "Thou art Christ, the Son of the living God." Jesus accepted this clear profession of His divinity as He answered, "Blessed art thou Simon, Bar-Jona, for flesh and blood has not revealed this to thee, but my Father in heaven. And I say to thee, thou art Peter, and upon this rock I will build my Church, and the gates of hell shall not prevail against it . . ." (Mt. 16:13 ff.).

Before the High Priest

Jesus is brought to trial before Caiphas, the high priest. Since the testimony of the witnesses does not agree, Caiphas turns to

Jesus with this solemn question, "I adjure thee by the living God that thou tell us whether thou art the Christ, the Son of God." Jesus answers with equal solemnity, "Thou hast said it," which is the same as saying: I am. And enlarging on what He has said He continues, "Nevertheless I say to you, hereafter you shall see the Son of man sitting at the right hand of the Power of God and coming upon the clouds of heaven." The words of Jesus are unmistakable and the high priest rends his garment as he cries out, "He has blasphemed; what further need have we of witnesses? . . . What do you think?" And they answered and said, "He is liable to death" (Mt. 26:63 ff.).

The strength of Christ's testimony lies in the fact that He wrought countless miracles during His life, that He rose from the dead, and that the Catholic Church in her victorious march through the centuries is a standing proof of the truth of Christ's prophecy that the gates of hell shall not prevail against her.

Conclusions

If Christ is God, then His teaching is true and final. It is not theory or opinion that might be overthrown by the progress of science. But then, all views of life, all systems of philosophy contrary to the teaching of Christ, are utterly and hopelessly false.

If Christ is God, then His law is binding on all. His commandments are not mere counsels that may be accepted or rejected at pleasure. His authority is universal and every knee must bend to Him, not only the masses of the people, but also all governments and public institutions. If Christ is God, then no power on earth has the right to interfere with the work of the Church, to limit or control her in the mission given her by Him. Then the authority of the Church is supreme in all matters of faith and morals; she is the divinely established court to pronounce on the moral aspects of all human affairs and not confined to teaching a few pious practices to the faithful.

If Christ is God, then in Him alone can salvation be found. There is no other name given us by which we can be saved. No man will be forced in this life to submit to His authority; each one must make his choice for or against Him freely, but upon this choice his eternity depends.

St. Hilarion says that there is nothing more dangerous for the world than not to know and not to accept Christ. A world reduced to misery and chaos is in our days a tragic illustration of the truth of the saint's words. Under such circumstances the task of the faithful is clear. By a fearless profession of their faith in Christ, by their living deeds of faith, they must show the world the way back to Christ. "The more Thy divinity is attacked, the more we will profess it, O Heart of Jesus, in whom dwells the fullness of divinity."

16. HEART OF JESUS
In Whom the Father Was Well Pleased

TO DO the will of God and thus to please Him is the purpose of human life. To do so when the will of God binds under mortal sin is necessary for salvation; to do so in all things which God commands or desires is Christian perfection. Jesus, who not only taught us the ways of salvation but also showed us the ways of perfection, always did the things most pleasing to His heavenly Father. The Father was pleased with Him and gave solemn expression to His pleasure. He will be pleased with us also if we follow in the footsteps of our divine Saviour.

The Father Pleased

While St. John was preaching penance on the banks of the Jordan our blessed Saviour was among those who approached him asking for the baptism of penance. John was overwhelmed by the humility of the request and hesitated; he yielded, however, when Jesus said that it was necessary in order to fulfill the Scriptures, that is, the will of the Father. No sooner had Jesus been baptized than the heavens opened, the Holy Spirit came down upon Jesus in the form of a dove, and a voice was heard from heaven, "This is my beloved Son, in whom I am well pleased" (Mt. 3:17).

As the end of the public life of Jesus approached, at least three Apostles were to be especially fortified for the tests of faith that awaited them in the Passion of our Lord. Therefore Jesus took them with Him to a high mountain. All at once He was transfigured before their eyes. His face shone like the sun and His garments became white as snow; Elias and Moses appeared and spoke with Him. The Apostles were beside themselves with heavenly delight, and Peter thought of building three tabernacles, one for Jesus, one for Moses, and one for Elias, and then to dwell there forever. But whilst he was still talking a white cloud overshadowed them and a voice was heard out of the cloud, saying, "This is my beloved Son, in whom I am well pleased; hear him" (Mt. 17:1 ff.). Overawed, the Apostles fell on their faces, and when Jesus woke them up He stood before them again in the form of His lowliness. The memory of this event, however, lingered on in the Apostles and what it meant for their labors we can gather from what St. Peter wrote about it many years later. They knew that, doing the work of Christ, they were also pleasing to the Father; and even though their lives, like that of their divine Master, should end in suffering and death, the pleasure of their heavenly Father and the glory of their own transfiguration would be their reward exceedingly great.

Jesus Pleasing the Father

Jesus is pleasing to the Father because He is His Son, "the brightness of his glory and the figure of his substance" (Hebr. 1:3). In the divine nature of Jesus the Father sees His own infinite beauty, wisdom, power, and holiness; and in His human nature He sees the most perfect reflection of His love in the Sacred Heart of Jesus, the abyss of all virtues and the burning furnace of charity.

Again, the Father cannot but be pleased with Jesus when He receives the infinite glory which Jesus renders Him as the Head of the human race. Even though the least act of the Son of God carries in itself the full and adequate atonement for the sins of the world, nevertheless, in order to glorify the Father so much the more, Jesus offers Himself on the cross as the Lamb of God that takes away the sins of the world. Thus Jesus gives to the Father what men had denied Him and, even if they had never sinned, could not have given: infinite homage and glory.

Notwithstanding their sins, God loves men; they are the work of His hands, His children, and He longs to see them saved. Jesus fulfills this desire of the Father. By word and example He shows them the way to the Father and pays the price of their ransom in His blood. Even after His Ascension He continues in the blessed Eucharist to be their sacrifice and bread of life so as to insure their perseverance on the way of salvation. Must not the Father be pleased with Jesus when He beholds the millions of souls that are and will be with Him in heaven, saved through the work and the blood of His divine Son?

Our Way of Pleasing the Father

Through grace we become the adopted children of God, and the image of the Father is impressed upon our souls. We please the Father by guarding this image and perfecting it through the imitation of Jesus. Hence the Christian, eager to please the Father, will seek the glory of the Father in all things as Jesus did; he will submit to the will of God in all conditions of life, will accept and patiently carry the crosses of life as Jesus did.

In a very special manner we shall be pleasing to the Father, if we love our fellow men because they are the children of God. Love of neighbor is dear to our Blessed Lord. He speaks of it as a new commandment, as a sign by which men would recognize His disciples, and He accepts whatever we do to the least one of our brethren for His sake as done to Him. So intimately are the love of God and the love of neighbor bound together that the one cannot be separated from the other. St. John in a very straightforward way tells us that anyone who says that he loves

God, but does not love his neighbor, is a liar and the truth of God is not in him.

We can have no nobler and holier ambition in life than to be pleasing to our Father in heaven. Whatever may be our condition and state of life, our endowments of body and soul, the successes and failures of our work, one thing always remains possible: to love God and our neighbor. Yet love is the fulfillment of the whole law, all that God expects; love makes us pleasing to the Father.

17. HEART OF JESUS
Of Whose Fullness We Have All Received

THE words of this invocation are taken from the first chapter of St. John's Gospel. Having spoken of the majesty of the Word of God, that became man and dwelt among us, the Evangelist summarizes what he has said in these words, "And of his fullness we have all received" (Jn. 1:16). Jesus possesses all the perfections of the divine nature and all the gifts of grace of which human nature is capable, and through Him they are communicated to us. We will consider the three principal gifts by which we share in His fullness.

Adoption of Sons

All the fullness of the divinity dwells in the Sacred Heart of Jesus, because He is the Son of the eternal Father. At the moment appointed from all eternity He became the Son of Mary in order to make us the children of God. St. John tells us that He gave to all who believe in Him the power of becoming the sons of God. It is through baptism that this communication of sonship is accomplished. In baptism we are born again of water and the Holy Spirit, and the new life which we then receive is truly divine life. True, we are only adopted children, but divine adoption stands immeasurably above human adoption. Human adoption is an external relation which produces no change in the nature, life, or character of the adopted. Divine adoption produces a real internal change; we are raised to a higher order and receive an altogether new life. The same Holy Spirit that dwells in Christ now dwells in us also and gives testimony to our spirit that we are the sons of God. He becomes our guide as He was the guide of Jesus; but, again, as the Apostle says, "Whoever are led by the Spirit of God, they are the sons of God" (Rom. 8:14). Holy Church gives thanks for this great gift of the Sacred Heart, when on the feast of Pentecost she sings in the Preface, "Who, rising above all the heavens and sitting at Thy right hand, has today poured out the promised Spirit upon the sons of adoption."

Gifts of Grace

As children of adoption we share in all the gifts which the Holy Spirit has bestowed upon the Sacred Heart of Jesus. The prophet Isaias spoke of the Holy Spirit as resting on Jesus with the fullness of His seven gifts. As if to ratify and fulfill this prophecy, the Holy Spirit came down upon Jesus at His baptism. We too receive the Holy Spirit with all His seven gifts in baptism and in confirmation, since in Christ we are the children of God. When Jesus cried out in the Temple, "If anyone thirst, let him come to me and drink. He who believes in me, as the Scripture says, from within him there shall flow rivers of living water" (Jn. 7:38), He said this of the Holy Spirit, for until then the Holy Spirit had not been given, for Christ had not yet been glorified. In like manner we partake in all the other virtues and gifts of grace of the Sacred Heart. All the perfection and holiness of the saints in heaven and the just on earth is a participation in that fullness of the Sacred Heart of Jesus. Jesus is our life; He lives in us and we in Him.

Heavenly Glory

The gifts of grace bestowed upon us in this life are to prepare us for the yet greater gifts of the life to come. The blessed vision of God in heaven with all its bliss and glory is but a participation in Christ's vision of the Father. Faith and hope shall come to an end and we shall behold the Father, Son, and Holy Spirit face to face through what is called the light of glory. So wonderful is the splendor and transforming power of this light that it will change us into the likeness of God." Beloved, now we are the children of God and it has not yet appeared what we shall be. We know that, when he appears, we shall be like to him, for we shall see him as he is" (1 Jn. 3:2). On the day of resurrection the glory of the soul shall be communicated also to the body. Does not St. Paul tell us that in Christ we all have risen and that, if we die with Him, we shall also live with Him, and if we suffer with Him, we shall also be glorified with Him? Our body shall rise in the glory of Christ's glorified body; it shall be resplendent like the sun, beyond the reach of pain and suffering, independent of all material wants and needs. So the children of God shall be at home with their Father in heaven and enjoy the fullness of the gifts of the Sacred Heart in undisturbed peace and security forever. Our heavenly glory is the object of Christ's priestly prayer before His Passion, "Father, I will that where I am, they also whom thou hast given me may be with me; in order that they may behold my glory . . . and that the love with which thou hast loved me may be in them, and I in them" (Jn. 17:24 ff.).

Now that we have become children of God, let us walk worthy of our Christian dignity. Since we have received the gifts of the Holy Spirit out of the fullness of the Sacred Heart of Jesus, let us keep in touch with this Holy Spirit, that He may perfect in us the work which He has begun. And, while waiting for the final participation in the glory of the Sacred Heart, let us arouse within ourselves a great desire for heaven, for the coming of Jesus in glory. It was this desire that put the closing words of the Apocalypse upon the lips of the beloved disciple, "Come, Lord Jesus."

18. HEART OF JESUS
Desire of the Eternal Hills

BY THE eternal hills the whole of creation may be understood. It is eternal in the sense of everlasting, because it will not be destroyed but renewed and glorified at the end of time. The significance of Jesus, the God-Man, for all creation is stated by St. Paul when he writes to the Colossians, "He is the firstborn of every creature. For in him were created all things in heaven and on earth, things visible and invisible. . . . All things have been created through him and unto him, and he is before all creatures, and in him all things hold together" (Col. 1:15 f.). The God-Man is the first thought in the eternal decrees of creation; in Him and through Him created beings are to find their ultimate goal and perfection. Therefore Jesus is the Desire of the eternal hills, of heaven and earth, of angels and men and the whole irrational creation.

The Desire of Angels

Even without the sin of Adam the Son of God would have become man, according to the opinion of many theologians. The Incarnation of the Son of God was revealed to the angels and the adoration of the God-Man was the test upon which their future happiness was to depend. Many of the angels refused to adore and they were cast into the abyss. But ever since the moment of that revelation the good angels longed for the coming of the God-Man; their desire increased when man was created and they beheld the nature which the Word of God would assume. The Incarnation would be the grandest manifestation of God's wisdom, power, and love.

The Desire of Men

The story of the Fall of our first parents is well known. In punishment for their sin they were driven out of Paradise and heaven was closed to them. All seemed to be lost. But God's designs were not thwarted; His wisdom and love had prepared a more glorious restoration of what had been ruined by sin. God's promise of a Redeemer now became the star of hope that guided men in their misery. The sign of the Virgin Mother and her divine Son appeared on the horizon. Hope lived on and grew stronger among the patriarchs. Jacob blessed his son Joseph and the effects of this blessing were to last until the Desire of the eternal hills would come. Prophets spoke of Him; they described His life and death, the time of His coming. The desire for the Redeemer increased from century to century, even as the curse of sin exacted a heavier toll in the growing corruption of men. Isaias gave heart-stirring expression to this desire, and his words are heard to the present day in the Advent liturgy of the Church, "Drop down dew, ye heavens, from above and let the clouds rain the just; let the earth be opened and bud forth the Savior, and let justice spring up together" (Isa. 45:8).

Fulfillment

The Desire of the eternal hills appeared in that silent, holy night at Bethlehem. He brought forgiveness of sin and peace within the reach of all men of good will. But the final restoration of all things has to wait until the full number of the elect has been gathered from all nations and generations. Universal peace, the one fold and one shepherd, the ultimate, decisive defeat of the powers of darkness, is still far away. Today, in tear-filled eyes and in hearts afflicted with sorrow and grief, the desire is strong for the day when "God will wipe away every tear from their eyes. And death shall be no more; neither shall there be mourning, nor crying, nor pain any more, for the former things have passed away" (Apoc. 21:4 f.). From the night of bombed-out cities, from the darkness of prisons and death chambers, we hear cries and prayers for the time when night shall be no more. In the general poverty and destruction left by wars the desire grows so much stronger for that "incorruptible inheritance, undefiled and unfading, reserved for you in heaven" (1 Pet. 1:4).

Desire of Irrational Creation

Because the whole visible creation was called into existence for the sake of man, it also shared in the curse of man's sin. Thus ran the sentence, "Cursed is the earth in thy work . . . thorns and thistles shall it bring forth to thee . . ." (Gen. 1:17). The hills and mountains preceded man in creation and they witnessed the harmony and beauty of the beginning, the happiness of the first parents in Paradise; they also saw the ruin and misery which sin brought into the world. The curse of sin has overflowed upon the whole earth. It is not the original, God-willed state of nature that we behold now. But it shall be changed when all things shall be restored in Christ at the end of time. In the words of the great Apostle, "The eager longing of creation awaits the revelation of the sons of God . . . because creation itself also shall be delivered from its slavery to corruption into the freedom of the glory of the sons of God. For we know that all creation groans and travails in pain until now" (Rom. 8:19 f).

The Sacred Heart of Jesus will in due time eliminate every remnant and vestige of the curse of sin. He, the Desire of the eternal hills, is also our Desire. May He come soon and may men find eternal rest in His heavenly kingdom, in the fulfillment of all their desires: "And he will dwell with them. And they will be his people, and God himself will be with them as their God. . . . Behold I make all things new" (Apoc. 21:3, 5).

19. HEART OF JESUS
Patient and Most Merciful

PATIENCE enables us to bear the manifold adversities of life with peace of mind and full submission to the will of God. Mercy is sympathy and pity stirring in the heart at the sight of misfortune and helplessness, prompting us to relieve suffering; very especially it is charity toward the guilty, the ungrateful, and undeserving on the part of the very one who has been offended and has the power to punish the guilty. There was and there can be no greater guilt and wretchedness than that of sin, and there were not nor can there be greater sufferings than those endured by Jesus. The Sacred Heart of Jesus endured the sufferings in order to save the sinner and therefore He must have been most patient and merciful. See how He practiced these virtues during His hidden and public life.

Hidden Life

Jesus spent thirty years of His short life in the obscurity of Nazareth, earning His daily bread in the sweat of His face, while He could have enjoyed all the wealth and all the honors of the world. He could have relieved the poverty of His holy parents and of His countrymen and led them to a higher standard of living. Moreover, Nazareth was a small and insignificant town that could never attract the attention of the world. Why should Jesus spend so much time in such a place after He had come to save the world? And mankind was waiting for Him. He could have associated with the intellectual and spiritual leaders of the time; the depth and soundness of His argumentation would have

87

convinced them of the truth of His doctrines, and the charm of
His personality would have made them His enthusiastic followers.
He could have had the whole world at His feet. But God's ways
are not our ways. It was the will of the Father that Jesus should
spend that time in obscurity, and Jesus submitted patiently
and waited.

Public Life

Even more painful were the tests of patience during Jesus'
public life. His activity was confined to a small and insignificant
country, to a people that showed very little understanding for
the kingdom of the Messias, although their whole history had
prepared them for it. On the whole, the people with whom Jesus
had to deal were of a materialistic, narrow, nationalistic mentality.
Of course, they delighted in listening to Him, they were amazed
at the greatness of His miracles, they were impressed and charmed
by the goodness of His heart, and they flocked to Him and
brought along their sick to be healed. But they did not grasp
the deeper meaning of His doctrines and His miracles. They
wanted to make Him king after the miraculous multiplication of
the loaves, but before Pilate they rejected Him and called down
His blood upon themselves and their children. Even the Apostles,
in spite of their close association with Jesus, showed an astounding
lack of understanding for the ideas of their Master. On the eve
of His Passion they quarreled among themselves about which of
them would be the greatest, and on the way with Him to Mount
Olivet on the day of His Ascension, they asked Him whether He
would now establish His kingdom. Lastly, the leading classes of
the people, the high priests, priests, and scribes, were His bitter
enemies. They opposed Him at every step, spied on Him, mis-
interpreted His words, accused Him of breaking the law, of
blasphemy, of rebellion, and even of dealings with the devil.
They did not rest until they saw Him on the cross and, as they

thought, His name and work ruined. Yet Jesus bore all this with endless patience, without bitterness or complaint, and continued to do good. He saw in all these disappointments and persecutions the chalice which His Father had prepared for Him.

Most Merciful

The sinner has offended God and proved himself most ungrateful; he has abused the gifts of God and dishonored his greatest benefactor. He, who was formed out of the dust of the earth and is nothing whatsoever of himself, has defied his Maker. God holds the sinner in His hands; He could annihilate him, thrust him into the abyss of hell in the very moment in which he sins. Jesus is God, yet He does nothing of the kind. He has come to save, not to destroy. He lovingly calls the sinner to repentance, offers forgiveness, takes the punishment of sin upon Himself, and makes atonement for it in His blood. All that has been lost through sin and much more is placed within the reach of the sinner. And the price the sinner has to pay for such unheard-of goodness is nothing but a sincere change of mind, sorrow for his sins, and amendment of life, no matter how great or how numerous his sins may have been. Such was the mercy of the Sacred Heart of Jesus while on earth, such it is now in the sacrament of penance, and such it will remain to the end of time, as long as there will be sinners to save. There is no limit to the mercy of the loving Heart of Jesus.

The follower of Christ must also be patient and merciful. Life is filled with many miseries; by patience we can turn them into blessings. We can be patient and merciful toward the materially and spiritually poor and miserable who surround us on every side, ungrateful and undeserving as they may often be. Our acts of patience and mercy are the keys that will open for us the treasury of the Sacred Heart of Jesus, when we stand in need of His patience and mercy.

20. HEART OF JESUS
Rich for All Who Invoke Thee

WE CALL people rich if they possess an abundance of the wealth of this earth, money, lands, houses, factories, and the like; but we also speak of men as rich in virtue, knowledge, experience. In whatever sense we take the word, the Sacred Heart of Jesus is infinitely rich, and, what is of special interest to us, It is rich for us. While the rich of this world often guard their riches carefully, hold on to them tenaciously, and communicate them to others sparingly, Jesus is eager to distribute His riches lavishly to all who ask Him.

Infinitely Rich

Even the richest men of this world own only a very small portion of the wealth of the earth. Moreover, all their possessions are uncertain, depending upon many conditions beyond their control. Thousands of rich people have been impoverished in consequence of depressions and wars. And even the richest must leave it all behind in death. The riches of Jesus are not subject to such limitations and uncertainties. Because all things were made by Him, He is absolute and permanent owner and master of all things. His are all the gold and silver and precious stones, the coal and oil buried in the bosom of the earth. His are the grass of the meadows and the grain of the fields, the birds of the air and the fish in the water, all living beings on the face of the earth.

Besides all these material riches, Jesus has the spiritual riches of truth and grace. He knows all truth because He is the Truth;

He possesses all virtue, because He is the abyss of all virtues; He possesses divine immortal life because He is the Son of the almighty, living God. We see these riches of Jesus displayed in the doctrines of our holy faith and in the sacraments and blessing of our holy Church. It is these riches that St. Paul has in mind when he writes, "I give thanks to my God always concerning you for the grace of God which was given you in Christ Jesus, because in everything you have been enriched by Him" (1 Cor. 1:4 f.).

Invoking Jesus

Whereas the rich of this world are generally anxious to keep what they have, Jesus is most eager to let us share in His riches. The initial gift of prayer He bestows upon us even without our asking, and the amount of the gifts He offers is unlimited. "Ask and it shall be given you; seek and you shall find; knock and it shall be opened to you. . . . Or what man is there among you, who, if his son asks him for a loaf will hand him a stone? Or, if he asks for a fish will hand him a serpent? Therefore, if you, evil as you are, know how to give good gifts to your children, how much more will your Father in heaven give good things to those who ask him" (Mt. 7:11 ff.).

One thing must be borne in mind. Jesus is most eager to bestow His gifts upon us, but He will not grant our petitions when they would be harmful to our soul. A good mother will not give her child a loaded revolver or a bottle of poison, no matter how much she loves him nor how insistently the child may ask for it. Jesus is our Saviour; He cannot give us things that would ruin us. But He will give something else instead, something conducive to our salvation.

Material vs. Spiritual Riches

Jesus loved poverty and called the poor in spirit blessed. With all the goodness He showed to the poor during His earthly life, we do not read of a single instance when He bestowed material wealth upon a person, not even upon His holy Mother and His foster father. He Himself wished to be poor, poor in His childhood, poor in His public life, but poorest on the cross. Thus He impressed upon His followers the truth that material goods possess no value in themselves, that they have been created solely for the purpose of assisting us in saving our souls and that only for this purpose should they be asked for.

On the other hand, Jesus is most eager to bestow spiritual riches upon us. The very fact that He revealed His Sacred Heart to us proves His eagerness to share the gifts of His love. The wonderful promises He made to St. Margaret Mary for all those who would foster devotion to His Sacred Heart cannot but fill our souls with grateful joy and unlimited confidence. We are assured of all graces necessary for our state of life, peace in our homes, comfort in affliction, special assistance in the hour of death, forgiveness and mercy for our sins, blessing for our undertakings, spiritual fervor, our names written in His Sacred Heart forever.

Convinced of this love of the Sacred Heart, we will gladly leave it to Him to answer our petitions as He sees fit. If our prayers, especially for temporal favors, are not heard, we will know that what we asked was not for the best, and that we shall receive something better, an increase of His grace and love which brings with it an increase of heavenly glory, the essence of which is the possession of Him who is our God and our All.

21. HEART OF JESUS
Source of Life and Holiness

ALL life, natural as well as supernatural, has its source in the Sacred Heart of Jesus, because it is the Heart substantially united to the Word of God, of whom St. John says, "All things were made through Him, and without Him has been made nothing that has been made" (Jn. 1:3). Now we will consider only supernatural life, which is the life of sanctifying grace. This life, inasmuch as it is a participation in the divine life, is also holiness. That is why, in early times, the faithful who had been sanctified through baptism were called saints. The Sacred Heart of Jesus is the source of all supernatural life and of every degree of holiness.

Life

In the Easter Preface, holy Church states that Jesus by His death has overcome death and by His Resurrection has restored life. The death which He has overcome is the death of sin; the life which He has restored is the life of grace and heavenly glory. At the Last Judgment the body shall rise and share in this life of the soul. The manner in which this life is communicated to us has been wonderfully illustrated by our Lord Himself in the parable of the vine and the branches. He says, "As the branch cannot bear fruit unless it remain on the vine, so neither can you, unless you abide in me. I am the vine, you are the branches. He who abides in me and I in him, he bears much fruit; for without me you can do nothing. If any one does not abide in me, he shall be cast out as the branch and wither; and they shall

gather them up and cast them into the fire and they shall burn"
(Jn. 15:4 ff.). It is the same sap that flows in the vine and in the
branches, the same life that is active in both. Thus Christ, the
divine vine, with His roots in the divinity, has grafted us on
Himself as branches and now sends forth His own life and fruit-
bearing power into us. But we remain living branches only as
long as we remain united to Him. Separated from Him, we are
dead spiritually and our lot is to be burned in the fire of hell.
It is for this reason that holy Church prays with such tender
solicitude in her preparation for Holy Communion, "Deliver me
through this Thy most sacred body and blood from all my iniquities and from all evil, make me always cleave to Thy commandments, and never suffer me to be separated from Thee."

Holiness

Supernatural life is given to the soul in an incipient stage and
now it must develop and grow. To keep alive, the human body
must be active, the lungs must breathe, the heart must beat,
the blood must circulate, food must be assimilated. The same
holds for the supernatural life; according to the vigor and intensity
of its operations, we are holy in a lesser or higher degree. Holiness
consists in hating what is evil and loving what is good. What
these things are in particular God has made known to us in His
commandments and counsels, and we share in His holiness to the
extent that we avoid what offends Him and do what is pleasing to
Him. Holiness is indeed nothing else but the practical conformity
of our will with the will of God. "He who has my commandments
and keeps them, he it is who loves me" (Jn. 14:21).

To hate evil we must know its malice, and to love the good
we must be aware of its beauty and blessings, but before we can
do these things the weakness of our nature must be strengthened
by the power of grace. That strength comes to us through the
Sacred Heart of Jesus. In His Passion, Jesus demonstrated the

malice of sin. His humiliations were punishment and atonement for the pride of sin. The cruel tortures inflicted upon Him were punishment and atonement for sinful pleasure. Prayerful meditation on the Passion will arouse a deep and lasting hatred of sin. On the other hand, love for what is good will be enkindled by reflection on the beauty and grandeur of His holy life as He places it before us in His teaching and example. Jesus always does the things most pleasing to the Father, and that is the highest degree of holiness. He is the holiest of the holy but He calls on us to learn of Him, to do as He has done, to love as He has loved. And even though human weakness may be great, His grace is all-powerful; strengthened by His grace, we can do all things.

At the Source

The loving Heart of the Saviour offered us the help we need. "Come to me," He said, "all you who labor and are burdened and I will give you rest. Take my yoke upon you and learn from me, for I am meek and humble of heart; and you will find rest for your souls. For my yoke is easy and my burden is light" (Mt. 11:28 f.). Prayer keeps us close to Jesus; it illuminates the mind and warms the heart, lifts thoughts and desires heavenward and thus lightens the burdens of the Christian life. In holy Mass we share in the atoning power of His Passion and learn the lessons of a holy life: profound reverence for the majesty of the Father, humility, obedience, and patience. In Holy Communion our whole being is more strongly and deeply penetrated with His divine life. "He who eats my flesh and drinks my blood, abides in me and I in him. As the living Father has sent me and I live because of the Father, so he who eats me, he shall also live because of me" (Jn. 6:57 f.).

Jesus has come that we might have life and have it more abundantly. Through His death He has merited it, through His words and example He has made it known to us, through incorporation into Him He conducts it into our souls and makes us live in Him and by Him. Thus all grace and holiness has its source in the Sacred Heart of Jesus. If then we are eager to possess divine life and increase it in our souls, we know where to find it, "Abide in me and I in you. . . . Abide in my love" (Jn. 5:4, 10). All the saints without exception give testimony with St. Paul that, "It is no longer I that live, but Christ lives in me" (Gal. 2:20).

22. HEART OF JESUS
Propitiation for Our Sins

ST. JOHN, the beloved disciple, gave us the words of the above invocation, "My children, these things I write to you that you may not sin. But if any one sins, we have an Advocate with the Father, Jesus Christ, the Just; and he is a propitiation for our sins, not for ours only, but for those of the whole world" (1 Jn. 2:1 f.). St. John returns to the same idea in the fourth chapter of the same epistle, when he speaks of the great love of God, who has loved us first and "sent his Son, a propitiation for our sins" (1 Jn. 4:10). The Sacred Heart of Jesus is the propitiation for our sins because He restored to the Father the honor which men had refused to render, paid our debts, and merited for us the Father's friendship and adoption as sons.

Honor Restored

God, our Creator, Lord, and Father, surely deserves honor, and He has made the fact known in the Ten Commandments. Observance of the commandments honors Him. Yet men refused to give God this honor, and by way of punishment God allowed them to fall into idolatry. This was a most shameful degradation of man, since it gave the honor due to the one true God to gods and goddesses of his own making. The progress of civilization, it is true, has done away with crass idolatry among the vast majority of men, but it has not brought mankind back to the worship of God. Now a subtle, disguised idolatry has stepped into the place of the ancient worship of gods; it is the idolatry

97

of race and nationality, of wealth and power, of pleasure and
unrestrained liberty. Never before in the history of the world,
have we witnessed as in our days such deification of men who,
according to Christian standards, are criminals and moral out-
laws. The Sacred Heart of Jesus is the propitiation for all this
dishonor offered to God. His whole life, His teachings, His
miracles, His sufferings have for their object the honor of the
Father. "I have glorified thee on earth; I have accomplished the
work that thou hast given me to do" (Jn. 17:4). And since Jesus
is God, the honor He renders to the Father is of infinite value,
making full and adequate reparation for the dishonor of sin.

Debts Paid

Stronger than any human claims upon the services of other
men are the claims which God has upon our service, since all
we are and possess belongs to Him. By our very nature we are
the servants of God, bound to use the gifts which He has
bestowed upon us according to His will. However, we have not
done this. We have rendered service to the prince of this world
and made ourselves his slaves; our time and God-given faculties
have been squandered and the gifts of God abused. We con-
tracted an immense debt in this way, a debt so great that we
could never have paid it by ourselves. But the loving Heart of
our Redeemer became our propitiation by paying this debt in
our place. According to the prophet Isaias He was the great
servant of God. Jesus Himself declared, "I have come down from
heaven, not to do my own will, but the will of him who sent me"
(Jn. 6:38). And St. Paul writes of Jesus, "He emptied himself,
taking the nature of a slave and being made like unto men. And
appearing in the form of man, he humbled himself, becoming
obedient unto death, even to death on a cross" (Phil. 2:7 f.).
Jesus rendered service to make up for our failure. He served
in poverty and humility, in His teaching and miracles, in His

agony and death. Thus our injustices were rectified, our debts paid, and right order restored.

Friendship and Adoption

By nature we were children of wrath; through Jesus we have again become the children of God's love. As holy Church sings in the Easter Sequence, "The Lamb has reconciled sinners to the Father." Through the propitiation rendered by Christ we have again been made partakers in the divine life, and endowed with the most precious divine gifts. What was hidden from the beginning and unknown to our first parents, even in their original innocence, has been revealed to us. Through the mysteries of faith we have been introduced into the family secrets of God. And yet, wonderful as the light of faith is, compared to the darkness of paganism, it is but shadow compared to the light of glory that awaits us in heaven.

The yearning of the human heart for God and family and home and friendship has been satisfied. God is again the beloved Father of His children, and the closer they come to Him the closer they come to one another, the more they love one another. What a difference between the cold and selfish spirit of the world and the warm and cheering spirit of love that animates the children of God. But no matter how generous and blissful this mutual love may be, as long as we are in this life human imperfections and shortcomings will enter into our mutual relations. The full fruits of our Saviour's propitiation, the perfect blossoming forth of the love of the children of God, is reserved for the life to come. Then our Saviour's prayer will come true: "And the glory that thou hast given me, I have given to them, that they may be one, even as we are one. I in them and thou in me, that they may be perfected in unity, and that the world may know that thou hast sent me, and that thou hast loved them, even as thou hast loved me" (Jn. 17:22 ff.).

Where sin abounded mercy has abounded more. When at last faith shall be changed into vision, hope into possession, and love has entered its final and beatific stage, then we shall sing the mercies of God forever and ever. This is full reparation of all that was wrong, restoration of all that was lost, bestowal of gifts never thought of, propitiation beyond measure, and we owe it to the Sacred Heart of Jesus.

23. HEART OF JESUS
Loaded Down With Opprobrium

THE wisdom of God ordained that all those elements which constitute the malice of sins should have their corresponding punishment in the propitiation made by the Sacred Heart of Jesus. The pride of sin is atoned by humiliation, sensual pleasure by the terrible sufferings of the Passion, disobedience by obedience unto death, the narrowness and selfishness of sin by the piercing and opening of the Saviour's Sacred Heart. These features in the atonement of sin form the object of the following invocations of the litany. The root and beginning of all sin is pride, and in atonement Jesus suffered every kind of humiliation and abuse throughout His life but especially during His Passion. It will be enough to recall the incidents; the lessons to be derived are self-apparent.

Taken Prisoner
Betrayed by a faithless Apostle, Jesus is taken prisoner and led in chains to the palace of the high priest. The modern counterpart of the event would be a man handcuffed and led by a squad of policemen to police headquarters. Even hardened criminals feel the humiliation. What must be the feeling of a man in high station, innocent of any crime, highly respected in the community, under such circumstances.

Struck in Face
Jesus stands before the high priest. As the testimony of the witnesses does not agree, the high priest, against the provisions

of the law, calls upon Jesus to defend Himself or to admit His guilt. Jesus calls the attention of the high priest to the illegality of the question; guilt must be proved by the accusers. No sooner has He finished than a soldier strikes Him in the face. We shudder at the very thought of such an indignity inflicted upon the Son of the almighty God.

Mocked by Soldiers

After the caricature of a trial before the high priest, Jesus is given into the custody of the soldiers for the rest of the night. The soldiers look upon Him as a fool, a dreamer, a man with an unbalanced mind. So they play with Him as naughty boys might play with a drunken man or an idiot. They play prophet with Him, blindfolding Him and slapping Him in the face, and then calling upon Him to guess who struck Him. They renew their cruel sport the next morning after Jesus had been scourged. Now they play king with Him. They clothe Him with an old purple cloak, put a reed into His hand as a scepter, put a crown of thorns upon His head, and then march around Him, genuflecting in derision and mockingly saluting Him, "Hail, king of the Jews." Hell is jubilant; angels are horror-struck at the sight.

Barabbas

Pilate sees at once that Jesus is innocent; he would like to set Him free. Yet, he lacks the courage of his conviction, and, above all, he is the politician who looks to his own advantage. He thinks he has found a way out of the difficulty when he remembers Barabbas. This man is a notorious murderer and now in prison. According to Jewish custom the people may ask at Easter for the release of one prisoner. So Pilate gives them the choice between Jesus and Barabbas. Whom will they choose? The mere fact of being thus associated with a criminal and murderer is an unspeakable humiliation for Jesus, but the climax of the ignominy is that Barabbas should be preferred to Him.

Scourged

Failing to free Jesus, Pilate makes use of another expedient which, he hopes, will satisfy the Jews and save His life. He has Jesus scourged, that is, whipped publicly and in such a cruel manner that the sight of Jesus might arouse the pity of the Jews. Of course, a man thus scourged will be ruined socially for the rest of his life, and perhaps in health. After suffering this punishment Jesus would cause the Jews no further trouble. Behold, then, Jesus, most worthy of praise, "despised and the most abject of men" (Isa. 54:3).

Crucified

Finally Jesus is condemned to die on the cross, the most painful and most disgraceful death penalty. If ever a man arouses our sympathy it is when he is in pain and agony of death. There is no such sympathy shown to Jesus dying on the cross. Even in His death agony the Jews taunt Him with their mockeries and insults, "He has helped others, himself he cannot help. . . . Well, well, did you not say that we could destroy the temple and you would build it up in three days? Come down from the cross and we will believe in you. . . . He has called upon Elias; let us see whether Elias is going to save Him." The Sacred Heart of Jesus is a human heart; He feels the cruelty of these mockeries.

Aggravating Circumstances

To appreciate more profoundly the humiliations of Jesus we must add a few considerations. Jesus is known throughout the country, admired by the people as a great prophet and miracle worker. Has He now been unmasked as a fraud and impostor?

Add to this that it is Easter, and hundreds of thousands of people from all parts of the world have come to Jerusalem. They will take the report of what they have witnessed to their home countries and the first news that these countries will receive will be about a man who was crucified because of blasphemy and rebellion.

How the Heart of Jesus must have shuddered under the impact of these humiliations. Thus He atoned for the pride of sin.

In one of the apparitions of the Sacred Heart to St. Margaret Mary, Jesus complained about the coldness and indifference of so many souls, even of those consecrated specially to Him. Such indifference implies disregard and contempt of the love of His Sacred Heart and adds to His opprobrium. We must not become guilty of it. The best way of showing our gratitude for the humiliations Jesus endured for us is to bear humiliations patiently for His sake. There is no better way of atoning for the pride of our sins or of sharing in the atoning power of Christ's opprobrium, no better way of escaping the opprobrium of eternal damnation. Sharing now in the humiliations of the Saviour's Heart we shall also share in His heavenly exaltation.

24. HEART OF JESUS
Bruised for Our Offenses

IN A prophecy of the Passion of Christ we get a description of what is meant by the present invocation. "There is no beauty in him nor comeliness; and we have seen him, and there was no sightliness that we should be desirous of him . . . and we have thought him as it were a leper, and as one struck by God and afflicted. But he was wounded for our iniquities, he was bruised for our sins; the chastisement of our peace was upon him and by his bruises we are healed" (Isa. 53:2 f.). The body and its faculties are abused in sin and this abuse is atoned by the bodily sufferings of our Lord. Let us look up to Him hanging on the cross and there behold the work of sin.

The Body Lacerated

The scourging Jesus suffered was administered by a whip made of leather thongs, to which small iron hooks or pieces of lead or wood were attached. The effect of the punishment was so terrible that the victim frequently died on the spot or remained broken in health for the rest of His life. Now since Pilate ordered the scourging of Jesus to arouse the pity of the Jews and to save Him from crucifixion, it was particularly cruel. As the blows fell upon the body of Jesus, the skin began to swell and break, blood oozed out, increasing in volume until it actually streamed down to the ground. As the lashes were lifted for a new stroke they showed red, dripping with the Saviour's blood; pieces of skin and flesh adhered to them and were scattered about the

105

place. Indescribable pain raged through His body and forced tears
into His eyes and gentle moans from His lips. It is of this
lacerated body that we must think when we look upon the
crucifix. Thus Jesus atoned for the abuse of the body in sinful
pleasure, particularly the sins of the flesh.

The Head Crowned With Thorns

A special torture was devised for our Saviour's sacred head.
Jesus was crowned with thorns to ridicule His royal dignity. The
crown was made from a bush common in Palestine, which grows
large and sharp thorns. Branches of these were plaited together
and then tied around the head of Jesus in such a way that the
thorns would turn inside. The procedure must have caused Him
the most intense pain, and the soldiers increased it when they
took the reed from His hands and struck Him on the head. With
each blow the thorns pierced deeper into His skin, some even
injuring the bones of His skull; blood streamed into His eyes
and over His face and matted His hair into stiff, unsightly strands.
He wore the crown of thorns as He carried the cross; and the
crown remained on His head as He hung there for three hours.
All the while these thorns burned into His head, and the least
movement racked His whole body with excruciating pain. Thus
the Saviour's loving Heart atoned for pride and vainglory, for the
sinful display of fashions and the abuse of physical beauty in the
seduction of numberless souls.

Nails in Hands and Feet

The body of Jesus was fastened to the cross by means of large
nails. Crucifixion was considered the most painful of all punish-
ments and modern medical science agrees with this opinion. The
nailing itself must have caused unbearable pain. First the arms
were tied to the transverse beam of the cross and then the nails
were driven through the hand into the holes in the wood with

blows of a heavy hammer. The blood gushed forth profusely, the fingers bent and moved convulsively, and a sensation of burning spread through the whole body. The cruel procedure was repeated as the feet were nailed to the cross. The cross then was dragged to the place where it was to be raised and set into the ground. It went into place with a jerk that sent a quivering pain through every fiber of the body.

The agony of three hours followed. Merely to be suspended by the hands that long with ropes would be intolerable. Jesus was suspended, not with ropes, but with nails in His hands and feet. The blood still left in Him after the scourging could not circulate properly and a sensation of unbearable pressure on the heart was the result; the lungs breathed heavily, the face turned pale and blue, an intense thirst caused the mouth to open and showed the tongue parched and dry. Long ago the psalmist had foretold it all, "My strength is dried up like a potsherd, my tongue cleaves to my jaws, . . . They have dug my hands and my feet, they have numbered all my bones" (Ps. 21:16 ff.).

Thus Jesus atoned for the sinful pleasure procured by the abuse of hands and feet. The hands have been employed in deeds of violence and lust, they have torn down the temple of God and built monuments to human pride, they have amassed gold and silver to buy every pleasure the world could offer, but they have left the works of salvation undone. The feet have carried the sinner on paths of sin, but failed to walk on the narrow road that leads to heaven. Indeed, there is not a feature or element in sin for which the Heart of Jesus has not atoned.

Saints have called the crucifix their book. St. Philip Benizi on his deathbed asked for his book; he meant the crucifix. Clasping it to his heart he said, "This is my book, of all books the most precious and most cherished. In this book I read throughout my life; with this book I want to die." Jesus Himself directed St. Angela of Foligno to read in this book; from it she would learn the depth of His humility, the disgrace and bitterness of His Passion. In this book we too will learn most precious lessons. It speaks to us of the malice of sin and the greatness of our guilt; it teaches us to do penance and to love Jesus in return. In this book we find consolation in all trials, invincible strength in temptation, perseverance and life everlasting. And so, "It behooves us to glory in the cross of our Lord Jesus Christ, for in Him is our salvation, life, and resurrection; through Him we have been saved and delivered" (Introit, Holy Thursday).

25. HEART OF JESUS

Obedient Unto Death

EVERY sin is an act of disobedience; it is the following of one's own will in opposition to the will of God. The proper atonement for disobedience is obedience, and the Sacred Heart of Jesus has rendered it by becoming obedient unto death. "Just as by the disobedience of the one man the many were constituted sinners, so by the obedience of the one many will be constituted just" (Rom. 5:19). The whole life of Jesus is a long drawn-out act of obedience.

Life's First Moment

It is the common teaching of theologians that the soul of Christ had the perfect use of reason from the very first moment of its existence. The soul of Christ in the very moment of its creation beheld the Father, Son, and Holy Spirit in the beatific vision, and its own exaltation through the hypostatic union with the Person of the divine Word. It fully realized the purpose of this union, namely, to give to the world a Saviour who would be God and man at the same time. The thoughts and sentiments of Jesus in that moment were foretold by the prophet, and St. Paul quotes the words of the psalmist in his Epistle to the Hebrews, "Sacrifice and oblation thou wouldst not, but thou hast fitted a body to me. . . . Then said I, Behold, I come . . . to do thy will, O God" (Hebr. 10:5 ff.). The first act of the Saviour is an act of obedience and this obedient attitude never changes throughout His life.

Hidden From the World

Every event and circumstance in the life of Jesus was pre-ordained by the Father, and Jesus took them precisely as manifestations of His Father's will, which He had come to fulfill. So He welcomed His birth at Bethlehem amid circumstances which must have been extremely painful to His holy Mother and because of His Mother also to Him. Yet, He gave expression to the joy of His heart in the hymn of the angels which announced His life's program as He had accepted it, "Glory to God in the highest and peace on earth among men of good will" (Lk. 2:14).

Unintelligible from the human point of view is the fact that the Saviour of the world, the Giver and Restorer of life, must flee to Egypt to save His own life. But the Father had sent the message to Joseph, "Arise, and take the Child and his mother and flee into Egypt, and remain there until I tell thee" (Mt. 2:13). Jesus asked no question; He obeyed.

Jesus spent the greater part of His life at Nazareth, a small and insignificant village. The Evangelist characterizes this period of our Saviour's life by these simple words, "And he went down with them to Nazareth and was subject to them" (Lk. 2:51). A few words, but an eternity of thought and reflection will not exhaust their depth. God subject to men, the Creator to the creature, the All-wise to persons limited in their wisdom and judgment, even though they were the holiest persons on earth. And all this for a period of time far exceeding the length of time men remain under parental authority. But Jesus had come to do His Father's will and He obeyed.

In the Sight of the People

During the three years of His public life Jesus went about the country doing good, preaching, healing the sick, casting out devils, raising the dead to life. By His wisdom and power He astounded the people and by the charm of His manners He attracted them, so that they would flock to Him in crowds. But the spirit that animated Him in this work was the spirit of obedience to the will of the Father. He said to the Samaritan woman, "My food is to do the will of him who sent me to accomplish his work" (Jn. 4:34).

Obedience made Him go after the lost sheep and associate with sinners, repulsive as sin must have been to Him, the Holy One. The Pharisees were scandalized, but Jesus told them: "I came down from heaven, not to do my own will, but the will of him who sent me. Now this is the will of him who sent me that I should lose nothing of what he has given me, but that I should raise it up on the last day" (Jn. 6:38 f.). And again, "It is not the healthy who need a physician, but they who are sick. I have not come to call the just, but sinners to repentance" (Lk. 5:32). The Father's will is that all men should be saved.

In Suffering and Death

The most painful tests of obedience were reserved for the end of our Saviour's life. At the Last Supper, as He was about to begin His Passion, He told the Apostles why He must suffer: "That the world may know that I love the Father, and that I do as the Father has commanded me" (Jn. 14:31). About two hours later He bore the terrible agony. His human nature shuddered and shrank from the terrors of the Passion. Bathed in bloody perspiration He lay on His face and cried to His heavenly Father, "Father, if it be possible, let this cup pass away from me; yet, not as I will but as thou willest" (Mt. 26:39). It was the Father's will that this cup of suffering should not pass away, but that He should drink it to its very dregs. Therefore Jesus forbade the fiery Peter to resort to violence in order to defend Him, "Put up thy sword into the scabbard. Shall I not drink the cup, that the Father has given me?" (Jn. 18:11.) Obedient to the will of the

Father He allowed Himself to be betrayed, put in chains, scourged, crowned with thorns, nailed to the cross, and He persevered in the pain and agony of the cross until all was consummated. Then only did He bow His head and die.

Thus Jesus atoned by His obedience for the disobedience of sin. Disobedience is forgetfulness of God, self-exaltation, refusal to serve; obedience is forgetfulness of self, self-immolation, loving service. In this lies the atoning power of obedience, its greatness and glory. It does the will of God, which is infinitely wise and powerful and loving and holy. Nothing could be more perfect, more blissful, more meritorious, nothing stronger and more powerful. Therefore the obedient man shall always speak of victory, even though it be victory through death. In a time of the most widespread self-exaltation and rebellion against the authority of God, the Sacred Heart of Jesus, obedient unto death, shows us the way to a truly great, fruitful, holy life on earth and to the exaltation of the children of God in life everlasting.

26. HEADING OF JESUS
Pierced With a Lance

ST. JOHN relates the event to which this invocation of the litany refers, "The soldiers therefore came and broke the legs of the first and of the other, who had been crucified with him. But when they came to Jesus and saw that he was already dead, they did not break his legs; but one of the soldiers opened his side with a lance, and immediately there came out blood and water" (Jn. 19:32 f.). Thus the soldiers unknowingly fulfilled what had been foretold, "Not a bone of him shall you break." And, "They shall look upon him whom they have pierced" (Jn. 19:36 f.). We too wish to look up to Him whose Heart has been pierced and reflect on the profound mystery of the event.

The Mystery of Death

Besides the loss of the supernatural life of grace through the sin of our first parents, men also suffered the loss of their bodily immortality. "As through one man, sin entered into the world and through sin death, and thus death has passed into all men, because all have sinned" (Rom. 5:12). The most appropriate punishment of sin as the destroyer of life is death. Body and soul are separated in death; the very being of man is torn asunder. Body and soul are made for one another, are incomplete without each other; their separation means the end of man as a human being. Thus death atones for the separation of the soul from God through sin.

God is the life of the soul much more than the soul is the life

of the body. This blessed and life-giving union of the soul with
God was broken asunder through sin. Like the branch cut off
from the vine, so the soul cut off from God cannot live. Nothing
remains to the sinner but a remembrance of happier days with
an unquenchable thirst for their return. The Sacred Heart of
Jesus has quenched this thirst of the human heart; He has died
and through His death has restored to us the life of God with
all its bliss and happiness. This is now the life of grace; in due
time it will be the immortal life of the body.

Blood and Water

According to St. Ambrose the blood and water that issued
from the pierced Heart of the Saviour is the blood of our
reconciliation and the water of our purification. In the Old Testament the high priest alone entered the holy of holies on the
day of atonement, with only the blood of the victims slain before-
hand. This rite was to signify that heaven, the eternal holy of
holies, had been closed to men through sin. Jesus, our divine
High Priest, entered and opened heaven for us by means of His
own blood. The day of Christ's death is the atonement day of
the New Testament, and His blood is the blood of the new and
everlasting testament.

The blood is followed by water, the water of purification. That
we eventually may enter heaven we must be purified from sin
and animated with divine life. Baptism, which gives us the
beginning of this divine life, is the laver of regeneration, by which
through water and the Holy Spirit we are born again and made
the children of God. Waters of grace flow in abundant streams
from the opened Heart of the Redeemer in the other sacraments and they divide into numberless streamlets, flowing into
every nook and corner of the human being, purifying it, giving it
fertility and growth in good works. Now the thirst of the soul for

God can be satisfied. "As the hart panteth after the fountains of water, so my soul panteth after thee, O God. My soul hath thirsted for the strong and living God; when shall I come and appear before the face of God?" (Ps. 41:2.) This prayer of the psalmist is answered by our blessed Saviour pointing to His Sacred Heart, "If any one thirst, let him come to me and drink" (Jn. 7:37).

The Opened Heart

Commenting on the gospel text that records the piercing of the side of Jesus, St. Augustine says, "The Evangelist expresses himself carefully so as not to say: He struck or wounded His side, or something like it, but that he opened it. It was then that, as it were, there was opened to us the door to life, whence came forth the sacraments of the Church, the sacraments without which there can be no access to that life, which is the true life." It was His opened Heart that our blessed Saviour showed St. Margaret Mary Alacoque with flames of fire issuing from it. The opened Heart impresses upon us the greatness of the love of Jesus, the inexhaustible riches of His mercy. He has given us His life, His merits, His virtues, His all. He has given Himself and there remains nothing else that He could give.

"Come to me all you that labor and are burdened and I will give you rest" (Mt. 11:28). The Sacred Heart of Jesus pierced with a lance has thus become for us the fountain of life and holiness. Through the blood and water issuing from It we have been cleansed from sin and shown the way of grateful, joyous, strong, self-sacrificing love. Love is strong as death. "Many waters cannot quench charity, neither can the floods drown it; if a man should give all the substance of his house for love, he shall despise it as nothing" (Cant. 8:7).

As Love has opened this Heart, so love alone can enter it.

Should it be hard to love Jesus after such manifestations of His love?

> Thou, Saviour, cause that every soul
> Which Thou hast loved so well,
> May will within Thy open Heart
> In life and death to dwell. (Feast of the Sacred Heart.)

27. HEADER OF JESUS

Source of All Consolation

CONSOLATION suggests the idea of suffering and sorrow. "The life of man is filled with many miseries" (Job 4:1), and so there will always be such as stand in need of consolation. Unfortunately men frequently seek their consolation where it cannot be found, in things which only aggravate their trouble. The source of all true consolation is the infinite love of God, and that love burns in the Sacred Heart of Jesus. From this source men must draw consolation, joy, and peace.

Wrong Sources of Consolation

There are many who attribute their troubles to poverty. They do not have, and because of conditions cannot acquire, the means to secure the ambitions of their lives. They cannot buy what they desire in food, clothing, furniture; they cannot take care of themselves in sickness as people of means can do; they cannot give their children the education which they see others enjoying. They feel embittered and in their bitterness throw themselves into a mad chase for money, paying little attention to the means which they use to acquire it. Others there are, who would drown their sorrow in the maelstrom of pleasure. Alas, it is usually sinful pleasure. Here is one who in his trouble takes to drink and ruins himself, body and soul; another stoops still lower and seeks his comfort in the pleasures of the flesh, forgetting what the Apostle says, that "they who sow in the flesh, from the flesh also will reap corruption" (Gal. 6:8). Again, there are such as seek their

consolation in escape from the scene of their trouble, in a change
of job, residence, companionship. All these may succeed in forgetting their original sorrow, at least for some time, but in the
end they must agree with Solomon when he writes, "I said in
my heart: I will go and abound with delights and enjoy good
things. . . . And whatever my eyes desired I refused them not;
and I withheld not my heart from enjoying every pleasure, and
delighting itself in the things which I had prepared. . . . And I
saw in all things vanity and vexation of mind" (Eccles. 2:1 ff.).
Money, honor, pleasure, and worldly success leave the soul empty,
disillusioned, and disgusted. All these things cannot bring true
and lasting consolation, because they cannot satisfy the heart that
is made for God and restless until it rests in Him.

Mission of Jesus

Jesus is the Prince of Peace. His mission is a mission of peace
to men of good will, and therefore also a mission of consolation.
The Heart of Jesus Itself is filled with the peace of the Godhead
and is therefore the source of all true consolation.

It was on a Sabbath, in the synagogue of Nazareth. Jesus
attended the customary religious service and the people of the
town expected Him to address them. Jesus rose and the book
of Isaias was handed Him. He opened the volume and read out
this passage, "The Spirit of the Lord is upon me, because he has
anointed me to bring good news to the poor; he has sent me to
proclaim to captives release and sight to the blind; to set at
liberty the oppressed, to proclaim the acceptable year of the Lord
and the day of recompense" (Lk. 4:17 ff.). Jesus sat down again
and the eyes of all present were riveted upon Him. What would
He say now? Jesus told them that these words of the prophet had
found their fulfillment in Him.

True, the mission of Jesus was not in the first place one of
relieving bodily distress; the words of the prophecy must be

understood principally in a spiritual sense. But as all bodily suffering ultimately has its source in sin, so the healing of sin will also alleviate the suffering. Spiritual gifts, heavenly hopes and aspirations, therefore, will bring true relief, and Jesus offers them in His teaching and His example.

True Consolation

What better and more gladdening news could be given to the poor? Though they lack material wealth, they are rich in Christ, and there is no limit to the treasures which they can lay up for themselves in heaven. What greater consolation than to know that we can obtain forgiveness of all our sins, throw off the fetters of satan, and regain the liberty of the children of God? And no matter what may be the sufferings that afflict us, we can learn to bear them patiently and lovingly, when we remember that, "the sufferings of the present time are not worthy to be compared with the glory to come that will be revealed in us" (Rom. 8:18).

To the consolation of His words Jesus has added the consolation of His example. He has experienced all the grief and sorrow that could fall to the lot of man and suffered what no other man could endure. Labors, privations, disappointments, humiliations were His inseparable companions, and the cruel sufferings of the Passion stood before His mind all the days of His life. What a load of sorrow did He carry in His Sacred Heart until the dark night of His passion broke upon Him, beginning with His agony in the Garden. Jesus knows what suffering means and therefore His invitation to all that labor and are burdened to come to Him is full of understanding and sympathy.

Saints in Suffering

The wonderful effects of Jesus' consolation are visible in the lives of the saints. The more they love Him, the more they love to suffer with Him. St. Paul writes, "I am filled with comfort, I overflow with joy in all my troubles" (2 Cor. 7:4). St. Elizabeth, driven from her home with her three children during a cold winter night, goes to the near-by Franciscan monastery and has the monks sing the *Te Deum* in thanksgiving for the sorrow God had sent her. St. Magdalen of Pazzi prays, "O Lord, let me not die, but suffer." St. Theresa has no other desire but to die or to suffer. Such is the power and sweetness of the consolation that flows from the Sacred Heart of Jesus that sorrows can be changed into delight. Then, indeed, the yoke of Jesus is sweet and His burden light.

The Sacred Heart of Jesus has not changed and It is in our midst in the blessed Eucharist. If men would know the gift of God and seek relief from all their woes in this source of all consolation, the face of the earth would be changed, and happy faces would meet us everywhere.

28. HEADING HEART OF JESUS
Our Life and Resurrection

IN A former invocation of the litany we considered the Sacred Heart of Jesus as the source of life and holiness. We then understood life in its fundamental and primary meaning as the life of grace through incorporation into Jesus; holiness then implied growth and development of that life. In connection with the present invocation we wish to consider this life in its practical manifestations, in the sense in which the Apostle understands it when he writes, "It is no longer I that live, but Christ lives in me" (Gal. 2:20), or again, "To me to live is Christ and to die is gain" (Phil. 1:21). When can we speak of such a life? When we make our own the thoughts and intentions of Jesus, use the means which He used in their realization, and do it in the manner in which He did it. To the extent we share in this life of the Sacred Heart we also share in His Resurrection and glorified life.

Thoughts and Intentions

In the Introit for the feast of the Sacred Heart the Church applies to Jesus the words of the psalmist, "The thoughts of his heart are from generation to generation: to save their souls from death and to feed them in famine." The words stress the salvation of souls as the object of Christ's mission. He came down from heaven for us and our salvation, that we might have life and have it abundantly. It was the thought uppermost in His mind throughout His life. To save us from death and eternal damnation He died on the cross; in order to communicate that

new life to us He instituted the sacraments of baptism and
penance. Knowing that this world offers nothing that could
sustain and develop such a life and that the redeemed would
have to die of starvation if given no further help, He provided
for their spiritual sustenance. He fed their minds with the word
of His truth, filled their hearts with His love, and even gave Himself, His own flesh and blood, to be their food and drink in the
blessed Eucharist. To bring these His gifts to all succeeding
generations He founded the Church. And the solemn commis-
sion He gave to that Church was to preach the Gospel to all
nations, to offer up a clean oblation in His remembrance from
the rising of the sun to the going down thereof, to change bread
and wine into His body and blood to be the bread of life for the
children of God. If these thoughts and intentions of the Sacred
Heart are ours, the salvation of souls will have the uppermost
place in our minds. But then Christ is our life; we live in Him
and He in us.

Means to the End

The kingdom of Christ was not of this world. For this reason
the means which Jesus employed to carry out His intentions were
not the means used by aspirants to worldly success. The means
Jesus employed were prayer, humility, obedience, and work during
His hidden life, the preaching of truth and the practice of charity
during the years of His public ministry, and finally His self-
immolation in the bloody death on the cross. Never did Jesus
have recourse to the influence of wealth, the skill of diplomacy,
flattery to the great ones, compromise as to truth and justice.
So will he, in whom Jesus now lives, never have recourse to dis-
honesty, fraud, flattery, and compromise of principle. The less
he can do through external activity the more he will endeavor to
do through prayer and the intensity of his desires, his generosity

and self-immolation. If the cause of Christ does not progress as we would wish, the reason may well be that too much importance is attached to material means, to external display and worldly prestige.

Manner of Acting

Notwithstanding the labors and hardships of His life the Sacred Heart of Jesus at all times enjoyed profound peace in union with His heavenly Father. There was no haste, no worry, no excitement, no discontent; all was regulated by submission to the will of His Father. Self-possession and immersion in the peace of the Sacred Heart is characteristic of him in whom Christ lives. There is complete and absolute conformity with the will of God. God could hasten the extension of His kingdom, the conversion of the world, the suppression of His enemies; if He does not do so we should not become impatient. God is eternal; He can afford to wait. Let us wait with Him. Calmly, without worry or excitement, with the peace of the Sacred Heart in our hearts, we will accomplish the most for the cause of Christ in the world and in our own souls.

Risen and Glorified

Having been our resurrection from the death of sin and our new life here on earth, the Sacred Heart of Jesus will be our life in a yet more perfect manner in heaven. For, as the Apostle says, "What is sown in corruption rises in incorruption; what is sown in dishonor rises in glory; what is sown in weakness rises in power; what is sown a natural body rises a spiritual body" (1 Cor. 15:43 f.). Christ risen from the dead dies no more; in like manner death shall no longer have dominion over us after our resurrection from the dead. Death, with all its antecedents in bodily weakness and infirmities, in daily progressing physical deterioration, shall have disappeared. The body shall live in everlasting youth and vigor, unchanging and unchanged, because immersed in the inexhaustible fullness of the Saviour's glorified life.

The day of our resurrection is the day of our heavenly transfiguration. Like the body of Christ after His Resurrection, it will shine in undimmed splendor through all eternity. No longer is it an obstacle but the delight of the soul. It moves with the speed of spirits, it is where the soul wants it to be, it does what the soul wants it to do, with the ease and speed of the spirit. All this is the fruit of the love and work of the Sacred Heart of Jesus which is our life and resurrection. And so the words of the Apostle have found their glorious fulfillment, "For we were buried with him by means of baptism into death, in order that, just as Christ has arisen from the dead through the glory of the Father, so we also may walk in newness of life" (Rom. 6:4), in the newness of the grace and love of the Sacred Heart here below, in the newness of heavenly glory there above and forever.

29. HEART OF JESUS
Our Peace and Reconciliation

ANGELS sang a hymn of peace on the day our Saviour entered upon His mortal life, and on the day He began His immortal life He Himself brought the message of peace to His Apostles, "Peace be to you" (Jn. 20:19). It is the peace of the heart that has been delivered from the slavery of sin, the peace of security as to the future, the peace of friendship and perfect reconciliation with God. The Church gives joyous thanks for the gifts of this peace when she sings in the Easter Sequence, "Let Christians offer praise to the paschal Victim. The Lamb has redeemed the sheep, the sinless One has reconciled sinners to the Father."

Peace as to the Past

The greatest disturber of peace in human life is sin. There can be no peace without God; sinners have no peace. If there is anything that makes us feel uneasy and fearful as we approach the end of life, and with it the final account we shall have to give, it is the thought of sin. Peace can be restored to the soul only through forgiveness of sin, and it is this peace which we owe to the Sacred Heart of Jesus. The angel brought joyous news to St. Joseph, when he informed him of the miraculous conception of Jesus, "And she shall bring forth a Son, and thou shalt call his name Jesus, for he shall save his people from their sins" (Mt. 1:21). Jesus proved Himself to be this Saviour during His mortal life when He called sinners to repentance and forgave their sins. He wished to be this Saviour to the end of time and, therefore, after His Easter message of peace to the Apostles, He instituted the sacrament of penance, "Receive the Holy Spirit; whose sins you shall forgive, they are forgiven them, and whose sins you shall retain, they are retained" (Jn. 20:23). Who counts the millions of sin-laden hearts that rejoice in their new-found peace when after a humble and contrite confession they receive absolution from their sins? It is the peace of the Sacred Heart communicated through the words of the priest, "Go in peace, thy sins are forgiven thee."

Peace as to the Future

Sin has disturbed our peace in the past; who guarantees that it will not do so again in the future? To avoid sin we must observe the commandments, we must strive after Christian perfection. For fallen nature this is not easy; human weakness is so great. There is even the dread possibility that we might die in the state of sin and lose eternal peace. This thought may become a cause of anxiety and fear. But Jesus, our Saviour, does not do things by halves. In Him and through Him we can at all times keep our hearts in peace. He has merited grace to avoid all sins, to observe all commandments; He does not expect the impossible. He admonishes us to have confidence; as He has conquered the world so we shall conquer. He governs the world; and to those that love God all things work together unto good.

We must not forget that He in whom we trust is all-wise. He makes no mistakes in guiding us, no matter how complicated and unintelligible His ways may appear at times to our shortsightedness. He is the almighty God, for whom there can be no obstacle or interference; even human malice must serve His designs, and human weakness, strengthened by His grace, is more powerful than all the power of satan and the world. His wisdom and power often choose to confound what is strong by weakness, and the wisdom of the world by the folly of the cross. Defeat becomes

victory, failure success, the dark night of Calvary is followed by
the glory of Easter. But, above all, it is the love of the Sacred
Heart that gives us complete security as to the future. He has
loved us unto death, He has given Himself to us in the blessed
Eucharist to be our Victim and our bread of life. What could
He refuse after He has given so much? We have the same grounds
for hope and joyous confidence that inspired the great Apostle
to write, "Who shall separate us from the love of Christ? Shall
tribulation, or distress, or persecution, or hunger, or nakedness,
or danger, or the sword? . . . In all these things we overcome
because of Him who has loved us. For I am sure that neither
death nor life, nor angels, nor principalities, nor things present,
nor things to come, nor powers, nor height, nor depth, nor any
other creature will be able to separate us from the love of God
which is in Christ Jesus, our Lord" (Rom. 8:35 ff.).

Friendship Forever

And so we are reconciled to God; we are His friends again.
Between friends there is but one soul and one heart. At the
end of the beautiful rite of the ordination of priests the words
of Jesus, spoken to the Apostles, are addressed to the newly
ordained priests, "I will not now call you servants but my
friends; for you have known all things whatsoever I have wrought
in your midst." So all the faithful are the friends of the Sacred
Heart and have experienced His goodness in the gifts He has
bestowed upon them. What had been hidden from the beginning
of the world, Jesus has made known to us in the mysteries of
faith. How rich and soul-satisfying are the things we know about
the Father, Son, and Holy Spirit, the life and Passion of our
Lord, about heaven and the communion of saints. In Jesus all
those who have gone before us with the sign of faith, whether
they be in purgatory or in heaven, are our truest friends, their
friendship no longer subject to the changes of human fickleness;

they are ready to help even when we do not deserve their friendly service, because they love us with the love of Jesus' Sacred Heart. And then beyond the horizon of this life there beckons the final and everlasting reunion of all the children of God with no fear of any more disturbance or separation. Heavenly peace and joy will be the full fruit of the peace and reconciliation wrought by the Sacred Heart of Jesus.

Freed from sin, made secure against temptation and danger by the power of grace, friends of God — what could we fear? "There is no fear in love, but perfect love casts out fear" (1 Jn. 4:18). "May the peace of Christ reign in your hearts; unto that peace, indeed, you were called in one body. Show yourselves thankful" (Col. 3:15).

30. HEART OF JESUS
Victim of Sinners

THIS truth is daily proclaimed in holy Mass, that Jesus is the Lamb of God who takes away the sins of the world. Jesus died in place of sinners to atone for their sins. According to Isaias, "He was wounded for our iniquities, he was bruised for our sins; the chastisement of our peace was upon him and by his bruises we are healed" (Isa. 53:5). St. John, the Precursor, directs the attention of the people to Jesus with the words, "Behold the Lamb of God, behold him, who takes away the sins of the world" (Jn. 1:29). St. Peter, too, has the idea of the Lamb of God in his mind when he writes, "You know that you were redeemed . . . with the precious blood of Christ as of a Lamb without blemish and without spot" (1 Pet. 1:18). Let us consider the perfection of this divine Victim in the light of Its types, the Old Testament victims, and then in the actual offering of the sacrifice.

The Victim

In the oblation prayer that follows immediately after the consecration in holy Mass, Jesus, the divine Victim, is spoken of as the pure, the holy, and the immaculate Victim. The words refer to the law of the Old Testament, according to which only the so-called clean or pure animals could be used for sacrifice; these had to be perfect in every way, and sanctified by a special religious rite before their oblation.

Why only certain kinds of animals were admitted as victims

we do not know. The deepest reason, however, seems to be that compliance with such an ordinance was an act of obedience, and obedience is the most appropriate attitude in offering sacrifice. The purity of these victims was solely an external, legal purity, but it typified the moral purity of the divine Victim, "the brightness of the Father's glory and the figure of his substance" (Hebr. 1:3). Such purity can fully make up for the defilement of sin.

The victim chosen from clean animals for the purpose of sacrifice became holy unto God by this very choice; to this was added a special sanctification through the performance of a sacred rite. Jesus, the divine Victim, is chosen from all eternity, sanctified by the hypostatic union with the Person of the divine Word, anointed by the Holy Spirit with the fullness of His gifts — holy unto God in an immeasurably higher degree than all the victims of the Old Testament.

Victims chosen for sacrifice in the Old Testament had to be physically perfect and without blemish. Even physical defects are, at least in the wider sense, an effect of sin; yet, only what is free from any trace of sin is fit to be used in a sacrifice that is to atone for sin. Only He is absolutely without blemish who never was under the influence of sin, who always did the things most pleasing to the Father. Such a Victim is the Sacred Heart of Jesus, "holy, innocent, undefiled, separated from sinners, and made higher than the heavens" (Hebr. 7:26).

Led as a Sheep to the Slaughter

"He shall be led as a sheep to the slaughter and shall be dumb as a lamb before his shearer, and he shall not open his mouth" (Isa. 53:7). The Sacred Heart saw Calvary from the beginning of His life and in it He saw the Father's will. He allowed Himself to be led to it over rough and stony paths. He was led to Bethlehem and Jerusalem, to Egypt and to Nazareth by His holy Mother and St. Joseph. As He began His public life, He was led by the Holy Spirit into the desert to be tempted by the devil. Then we find Him under the guidance of the same Holy Spirit in the towns and villages of Palestine, among crowds of good and simple people who admired and loved Him, but also among the proud and hypocritical Pharisees, who hated Him and sought His destruction. As the end of His life approached, He allowed Himself to be led in chains to Annas and Caiphas, to Pilate and Herod, to Calvary, to die on the cross. All this He did without opening His mouth, "who when he was reviled did not revile, when he suffered he did not threaten, but yielded himself to him, who judged him unjustly" (1 Pet. 2:22).

Praying and Forgiving

If Jesus was silent in His own defense, He spoke so much the more in prayer to His heavenly Father. He prayed for those who hated Him and brought Him to His condemnation, He promised paradise to the repentant thief, He bequeathed to the world the greatest treasure of His Sacred Heart, His holy Mother, henceforth to be our Mother. He thirsted for the salvation of those for whom He died and suffered the agony of abandonment to atone for the sins of those who abandon God. Only when the Father's will was accomplished to the last detail did He commend His soul into the hands of the Father and give up the ghost.

Victim Souls

To benefit by the sacrifice of the divine Victim we too must be victims. From the above considerations we can learn how to do it. We must be victims that are holy and immaculate and pure. We become holy when consecrated to the service of God in baptism and confirmation; we are immaculate if we live up to this consecration, we remain pure through the avoidance of sin. Like the divine Victim we must conform our will to the will of the Father, always doing the things pleasing to Him, submitting humbly and lovingly to all the dispensations of Providence in our lives. Impatience and complaining take away the fragrance of sacrificial love. We ought to be victims not only for our own sins, but for the sins of the world. Never was there a greater need of sacrifice and atonement. Hence the urgent request of our Lady of Fatima for prayer and penance in behalf of sinners. This victim spirit should be the object of the prayers of the faithful, especially at holy Mass as we offer the divine Victim, holy and immaculate and pure.

31. HEART OF JESUS
Salvation of Those Who Hope in Thee

THE very name of Jesus means Saviour. St. Joseph is told to call His name Jesus, "for he shall save his people from their sins" (Mt. 1:21); the shepherds of Bethlehem are to rejoice because, "there has been born to you today in the town of David a Savior, who is Christ the Lord" (Lk. 2:11); Jesus Himself characterizes His mission as one of salvation when He says, "the Son of Man came to save what was lost" (Mt. 18:11). There is no other name by which we could be saved. However, Jesus is Saviour in point of fact only for those who accept Him as such, who hope in Him.

Salvation

Salvation implies deliverance from sin and death, perseverance in grace to the end, and life eternal. But only he who believes and is baptized shall be saved. And since it is the will of God that all men should be saved and Jesus died for the salvation of all, Jesus sends out the Apostles into the whole world to preach the Gospel to all nations and to baptize them.

Yet, faith alone will not save us. Saving faith is living faith. "Not everyone who says to me, 'Lord, Lord,' shall enter into the kingdom of heaven, but he who does the will of my Father in heaven, he shall enter into the kingdom of heaven" (Mt. 7:21). Doing the things God wants us to do is fulfillment of the great law of charity, and only love unites with God and saves. God demands the observance of the commandments and obedience

133

to the guidance of the Church and that to the end of life, for only "whoever perseveres to the end, he shall be saved" (Mt. 24:13). But constant observance of the commandments of God is beyond our strength.

Our helplessness is aggravated by the fact that there are evil influences within and without seeking our destruction. Satan and the evil spirits roam through the world seeking the ruin of souls. St. John speaks of the things that are in the world as the lust of the eyes, the lust of the flesh, and the pride of life. The human will has been weakened and the material element in man rebels against what is left of good and noble aspirations. The deceptive beauty and pleasure of material things exercise a disastrous influence over the mind and will of man; beautiful clothes and homes, food and drink and pleasure appeal to the senses and subdue the will. The flesh asserts itself in the most shameless and persistent manner; it clamors for gratification and drags man down to the animal level. Where shall we find the strength to overcome these dangers and temptations? The great Apostle gives the answer, "I can do all things in him who strengthens me" (Phil. 4:13).

Lastly, we must reckon with the possibility of faults and sins because of our weakness. Indeed, Jesus Himself reckoned with it and therefore He instituted the sacrament of penance. The Sacred Heart of Jesus is our peace and reconciliation. He spoke the word of forgiveness many times during His earthly life and He continues to speak that word through the priest in confession. Surely, Jesus is Saviour; He alone can save and He offers His salvation to us, but under this definite condition: that we hope in Him.

Hoping in Jesus

Hope is the firm expectation of all things we need for our salvation from the goodness of the Sacred Heart. Great as are the things which we must hope for, we have every reason to expect that they will be readily granted, because of the fidelity, power, and love of the Sacred Heart of Jesus.

Jesus in His love has promised all those things: "He who follows me does not walk in the darkness, but will have the light of life" (Jn. 8:12). If we remain in Him we shall bring forth much fruit, "He who abides in me and I in him, he bears much fruit; for without me you can do nothing" (Jn. 15:6). The eight beatitudes in the Sermon on the Mount would have no meaning, unless He makes them possible by His grace; the very closing words of this sermon imply the possibility of doing the things Jesus had commanded or counseled. He who hears His words and acts upon them will be likened to a wise man who built his house on rock.

Jesus has the power to do what He has promised. All power in heaven and on earth is in His hands. He can heal the sick and multiply the loaves; He can calm the storm on the lake and raise the dead to life. As to His sheep who follow Him, the Good Shepherd says, "I give them everlasting life; and they shall never perish, neither shall anyone snatch them out of my hand" (Jn. 10:28). Shall our salvation be harder for Him than the salvation of those millions of saints in heaven who have washed their robes in the blood of the Lamb and now, clothed in white garments with palms in their hands, sing forever the mercies of His Sacred Heart?

All doubt and wavering in our hope that might trouble us at times must disappear when we consider the boundless love of the Sacred Heart of Jesus. His love aroused the hope of the people so that they brought to Him the sick and the ailing, the blind and the deaf, the paralyzed and those possessed by the devil. He helped them all. What love did He not show for sinners; He had come to call sinners, not the just, to repentance. To the present day we feel the intensity of His love and His desire to help when we read His touching invitation, "Come to me all you who labor and are burdened and I will give you rest. Take my yoke upon you and learn from me, for I am meek and humble of heart; and you will find rest for your souls. For my yoke is easy and my burden light" (Mt. 11:28).

Expectation and trust must be joined to co-operation with the grace Jesus offers. Just as only living faith leads to salvation so only living hope, that shows the works of hope, will save us. Hope begins each day with fresh courage, no matter how disappointing the day before may have been; hope approaches the most difficult problems and tasks with courage, for it can do all things in Him who is all-powerful; hope does not fear or waver in strife and struggle with the powers of hell, because it trusts in Him who has conquered the prince of this world; hope rises undaunted even from the most regrettable faults, for the mercies of God are above all His works. Hope asks and knocks and seeks, and it receives all that it asks, finds all that has been lost, has the key to all the treasures of the Sacred Heart. Living hope rises into the heavens, to the very throne of the loving Heart of Jesus and there finds salvation.

And so we firmly hope that the Sacred Heart of Jesus will be our salvation. If the days are dark and stormy, if the waves of sin and worldliness threaten to engulf us, we act like the Apostles during the storm on the lake. We cry to Jesus, "Lord, save us! We are perishing" (Mt. 8:25). He will save us. In Thee, O Lord, I have hoped, I will not be disappointed forever.

32. HEART OF JESUS
Hope of Those Who Die in Thee

DEATH is the punishment of sin. We speak of the death struggle, the death agony, and by that we mean the resistance which nature opposes to death. Man fears death; he does not want to die. Yet the death of the Christian ought to be peaceful and a cause of holy joy. It is the home-coming of the child to meet the Father in heaven; it is the deliverance from sin and danger, and entrance into that eternal life where death shall be no more, nor mourning nor crying nor sorrow. Such it will be indeed for all those who die in the Sacred Heart of Jesus. Jesus, our Saviour, full of love and mercy throughout our lives, will not forsake us in the most decisive hour, the hour of death.

Dying in the Heart of Jesus

In an inspiring scene, St. Luke describes the death of St. Stephen. The holy martyr stands before the members of the high council who are bent upon destroying the fearless preacher of truth. Stephen, full of the Holy Spirit, looks up to heaven; there he sees the Son of God standing at the right hand of the Father. His thoughts are with his divine Master as they drag him out of the city to stone him. And while the stones hurled at him do their work, he prays for his enemies, just as Jesus had done on the cross, "Father, lay not this to their charge. Having said this he fell asleep in the Lord" (Acts 7:55 ff.). St. Stephen hoped and died in the Sacred Heart of Jesus.

To die in the Heart of Jesus means to die believing in His boundless mercy. We grasp His extended hand; His mercy is

137

greater than all our sins. Through His opened side we seek refuge in His Heart that was pierced for us; we make the last breath of our mouths, the last beat of our hearts the last acts of love for Him who has loved us unto death. To die in the Sacred Heart of Jesus means that like Him we accept death with full resignation to God's holy will, at the time and place He chooses, with all the pain and sorrow that may accompany it.

Life and Death

Man commonly dies as he lives. If we wish to die in the Sacred Heart of Jesus we must also live in Him. We must be united with Him through sanctifying grace, believe and hope in Him, love Him, not only in words but in deed. The sentiments we wish to have in death must be familiar to us in life. Now we must practice resignation to God's holy will in the trials and crosses of life; now we must bear with patience the tribulations which His love sends us; now we must dwell with our thoughts in heaven, keeping our eyes steadfastly on Jesus sitting at the right hand of the Father, and draw inspiration from the glory which He has in store for us.

Hope in Death

In time of death satan will redouble his efforts to ruin our souls. Though we have renounced him in baptism, he has not renounced us. The hour of death is his last opportunity to recapture what he has lost. In that awful hour the Sacred Heart of Jesus is the hope of the Christian. The soul about to depart from this world is His property. He has acquired title to it by His Passion and death and no man shall pluck it from His hands, no power of hell shall be able to ruin the soul as long as it clings to Him. He, the King of dreadful majesty, holds the keys to life and death; He opens and no one shuts, He shuts and no one opens.

Sin is no obstacle to the infinite mercy of the Sacred Heart of Jesus. He came to save sinners; He died for them. There is joy in heaven over one sinner doing penance more than over ninety-nine just who need not penance. In His pierced hands and feet and Heart is written the love which He bore us during life, and this love follows us to the end. This love of Jesus is our hope.

> Thou, who Mary didst forgive
> And who badst the robber live,
> Hope to me dost also give.

Hope in Him speaks from the soul-stirring prayers that the Church offers us for the dying, from the holy water with which we sprinkle the dying Christian, the crucifix, the rosary, the blessed candle we put in his hands. The last rites bring us forgiveness of sin and in the holy viaticum Jesus comes in person to conduct us into His heavenly kingdom.

Happy Death

To die in the Sacred Heart of Jesus is to have a happy death. Therefore the death of saints is so peaceful, consoling, inspiring. St. Aloysius, informed that he must die, intoned Psalm 121, "I rejoiced at the things that were said unto me: We shall go into the house of the Lord." The last words of the Little Flower were, "O my God, I love You." The grace of a happy death is the crowning grace of life, for it means eternal salvation. It is the object of one of the promises made to St. Margaret Mary for those who foster devotion to the Sacred Heart, especially if they receive Holy Communion on nine successive first Fridays. They will find in the Sacred Heart a sure refuge in the hour of death and die in His grace. It is sweet to die in the Sacred Heart of Jesus. Let us hope in this Sacred Heart in life that It may be our hope in the hour of death.

33. HEART OF JESUS
Delight of All the Saints

THE happiness derived from earthly things is transitory, just as
these things themselves are transitory, and transitoriness interferes with perfect happiness. But even if earthly joys were everlasting, they could not satisfy the human heart, because our
hearts are made for God and restless until they rest in Him.
Perfect happiness is found only in beholding God face to face
and possessing Him forever. It is the joy of the saints in heaven.
In this last invocation of the litany the Sacred Heart of Jesus is
called the delight of all the saints. St. Bernard, known for his
tender love of Jesus, wrote these beautiful lines,

> Jesus, the very thought of Thee
> With sweetness fills my breast;
> But sweeter far Thy face to see
> And in Thy presence rest.

What Jesus is for His friends on earth He will be in an immeasurably higher degree for them in heaven. There they shall
see Him face to face, love Him with their whole hearts, and in
turn be loved by Him eternally.

Beholding Jesus

The essential joy of heaven consists in the direct and immediate
vision of God, a vision so soul-satisfying, so thrilling and absorb-
ing, that it is called beatific. St. Paul writes of this vision, "We
now see through a mirror in an obscure manner, but then face

to face. Now I know in part, but then I shall know even as I have been known" (1 Cor. 13:12). St. John is filled with delight at the very thought of it, "Beloved, we are now the sons of God, and it has not yet appeared what we shall be. We know that when he appears, we shall be like to him, for we shall see him just as he is" (1 Jn. 3:2). We shall behold Jesus in the glory of His divinity, the beauty ever ancient, ever new. Never shall we be able to exhaust the depths of its delights.

Next to the vision of His divinity, it is the sight of Jesus' glorified humanity that fills the saints with unspeakable delight. The beauty and charm of Christ's person attracted crowds of people to Him even during His earthly life. For a few moments He allowed the glory of His divinity to break through the veil of His mortal body on Mount Thabor, and the three Apostles who witnessed the event were overwhelmed by the delight of the vision. Peter did not know what he was saying when he spoke of building three tents so that they might stay there forever. In heaven the glory merited by His life and Passion are added. The marks of His wounds sparkle with the ruby luster of His blood and the diamond brilliance of His love. Now the saints see what a Master they served on earth. Once they thought of Him in the form of a servant; now they see Him in the form of God. Once they thought of His poverty and lowliness as their inspiration and encouragement; now they behold the inexhaustible riches of His divinity. Once they strove to imitate Him as meek and humble of heart; now they behold Him in the majesty of His eternal kingship, the King of kings and the Lord of lords.

Loved by Jesus

The human heart thirsts for love. Knowledge of being loved brings happiness, gives courage, consoles in adversity. The Sacred Heart of Jesus loves us with eternal love. As long as we are

in this life His love cannot reveal itself completely. We are still
in the stage of probation and the full manifestation of His love
would change this earth into paradise. But when the time of
probation has come to an end, all restraints will disappear. He
will show Himself to us face to face to reward our faith. He
will give Himself with all that He is and has to reward our
hope. He will bestow heavenly wealth for earthly poverty, joy for
pain, rest for labor, light for darkness, security for doubt and
uncertainty. Now the love of friendship has reached its final
stage, "My Beloved to me and I to him" (Cant. 2:16). We are
heirs of heaven and coheirs with Him and the torrents of
heavenly delight shall never cease to flood our hearts.

Loving Jesus Forever

As the eye is made to see, the ear to hear, the tongue to
speak, so the heart is made to love. Therefore the great commandment of the love of God, as it is man's foremost obliga-
tion, is also his only way to happiness. On earth the love of God
is mixed with sorrow, because human weakness interferes with
the full surrender of self that love calls for. As we advance in the
love of God the thought of our sins and the sins of others,
the squandering of love on things not deserving it, is a source of
disillusionment and grief. All earthly interferences with our happiness in loving God come to an end in heaven. Without sin
or temptation, without ever weakening, we shall give Him our
whole love in undisturbed peace and security.

With Angels and Saints

With supreme delight the saints now see Jesus loved and
honored by the Father and the Holy Spirit, adored and glorified
by all the saints. His honor and exaltation is also theirs; He is
their Beloved for whom they lived and labored on earth. And in
Him they also love one another with perfect love. Jesus is the

friend of each and every one of them. He is proud of them, proclaiming their love and loyalty before His heavenly Father and all the heavenly hosts. And so through the heavens resounds the canticle of joy and jubilation, "Salvation belongs to our God who sits upon the throne and to the Lamb. . . . Amen; blessing and glory and wisdom and thanksgiving and honor and power and strength to our God forever and ever" (Apoc. 7:10 ff.).

If we wish the Sacred Heart of Jesus to be our delight in heaven, we must seek our delight in Him already in this life. Let it be joy for us to think of Him, to speak of Him, to work for Him, to suffer for Him. The service of Jesus calls for labor and self-immolation, but love feeds on sacrifice. In suffering for Jesus the saints have found delights of which the world has no idea, and heavenly sweetness that they would not exchange for all the pleasures of the world. Imagine the Sacred Heart of Jesus addressing to us the words of the *Imitation of Christ*, "Be not discouraged because of labor undertaken for Me. It will not be long. . . . Be faithful; the day of peace and eternal rest will come, death and suffering shall be no more. If you had seen the crown of the saints . . . how you would long to work and to suffer; you would not complain. Therefore lift up your face to heaven. Behold, I and all the saints, who in this life had to fight a fierce battle, are now secure and at rest and shall be with Me forever in the kingdom of the Father" (Book I, Chapter 47). In the glorious kingdom of the Father the Sacred Heart of Jesus shall be forever the delight of all the saints.

Spare Us — Hear Us — Have Mercy on Us

THE litany began with a cry for mercy addressed to the three divine persons, and the same plea for mercy was repeated after each invocation. Now at the end of the litany the petition is directed to Jesus as the Lamb of God that takes away the sins of the world. The lamb as the most common sacrificial animal plays an important part in the sacred writings. The Old Testament paschal lamb was a type of Christ. As the slaying of the typical paschal lamb marked the deliverance of the Israelites from the slavery of Egypt and their departure for the promised land, so the slaying of the true paschal lamb upon the cross marked the deliverance of mankind from the slavery of satan and their departure for the heavenly land of promise. Isaias compares Jesus to a lamb that is led to the slaughter without opening its mouth. St. John, the Precursor, points to Jesus as the Lamb of God that takes away the sins of the world, and in the Apocalypse we see the Lamb enthroned in glory as the light of the heavenly city and acclaimed by all the saints as the author of their salvation. They all have washed their robes in the blood of the Lamb.

The closing petitions of the litany, therefore, sum up the fundamental truths of our redemption. We were saved through the blood of the Lamb of God. The divine majesty of the Saviour and His exceedingly great love for men, His life and labors and sufferings as well as the glorious fruits of His redemptive work have been placed before us in the litany. The love of His Sacred Heart has made Jesus the Lamb of God, that was slain for our sins. So we turn to Him once more at the end of the litany for mercy to secure for ourselves the fruits of His Passion: forgiveness of sin and amendment of life, perseverance in His love to the end.

Spare Us

Two ideas are suggested by this petition: suspension of punishment and time to repair the wrong done in the past. Jesus is our Redeemer, but also our Judge. We may feel that if we were to be judged now, we might not fare so well. Even though we might escape eternal damnation, judgment now might mean for us severe punishment in purgatory and a degree of heavenly glory far below what it could and should have been. We are determined to do better if given a chance. With the help of grace all that has been lost can be regained, and a high degree of sanctity attained in spite of a sinful or lukewarm past. Penitent saints prove the goodness of Jesus and the power of His grace. Now the sentence has not yet been spoken in our case and the mercy of the Sacred Heart is unlimited. So we beseech Him to spare us, not to judge us now, but to wait until we have done penance and acquired that degree of holiness which should be ours according to God's will. If our attitude in the past has been one of indifference, henceforth it is to be one of fervor; if it has been one of wavering and indecision, henceforth it is to be one of unswerving devotion and loyalty.

Hear Us

Even if granted a respite and determined to do better, we know that we need the help of grace in order to accomplish what we intend to do. All the invocations of the litany have impressed upon us our helplessness as well as the goodness of the Sacred Heart of Jesus. Therefore we wish to explain and to lay our needs and wants before Him as they arise. We want Jesus to listen to us, and that is more than merely sparing us. Even though a man may spare his enemy, not inflicting upon him deserved punishment, his attitude may become one of reserve and aloofness that excludes any other act of kindness. This we want to prevent. All the treasures of the world could not make up for the loss of the friendship of Jesus and the gifts of His grace, and heaven would not be heaven without Him. But the very fact that Jesus invites all those that are of heavy heart to come to Him is proof that He will gladly listen to any one who humbly and trustfully confides his troubles to His Sacred Heart.

Have Mercy on Us

Mercy is the fruit of love, doing good to one who stands in need of help although he does not deserve it. We surely have no claims on the gifts of God and therefore we appeal to His mercy. And what are, in particular, the gifts of love that we implore?

We need light, above all, to make us see the malice of sin and hate it as the greatest evil in the world. Unless we are determined to suffer death rather than commit sin, a closer approach to God is impossible. But the avoidance of sin alone does not make the perfect Christian according to the Heart of Jesus. There must be the love of virtue and the works of faith. Here we are faced with the danger that the attractions of the world may arouse worldly desires and choke off the love and desire for Christian perfection. The gift of mercy that we implore from the Sacred Heart of Jesus is a strong and persistent desire to become like unto Him, perfect as our Father in heaven is perfect. The wellspring of all idealism and holiness in the Christian life is love. Therefore St. Augustine can say, "Love and then do what you will." This, then, is the crown of all the gifts we implore from the Sacred Heart of Jesus; we wish to love Him who has loved us first, Him, who is the Lamb of God who died for us that we might live and love Him.

We are asking great things in these closing petitions of the litany, but they are not too great for the infinite love of Jesus. As the love of His Sacred Heart has delivered us from sin and its fearful punishment, so It lifts us up that through love we might become like unto Him. Thus the devotion to the Sacred Heart of Jesus has a profound significance for our cold, materialistic, selfish age. It is a call to selfless love, a powerful impulse to holiness of life. Let us close these reflections with the words of St. Margaret Mary, "I do not know of any devotion in the spiritual life more calculated to raise a soul to high sanctity in a short time and to enable it to taste the sweetness of the service of God. Yes, I repeat, if people knew how pleasing this devotion is to Jesus Christ, there is not a Christian who would not practice it."